MEMOIRS of a Fish Whisperer

DEAN ERTEL

Publishing Coordinator – Sharon Kizziah-Holmes

Paperback-Press
an imprint of A & S Publishing
A & S Holmes, Inc.

ISBN -13: 978-1-951772-77-2

DEDICATION

Dedicated to my uncle Gobe, who taught me how to fish, giving me a lifetime of joy and beautiful memories, and to my three children, Ben, Jenny, and Nathan. May they discover and enjoy their own lifetimes of hobbies and dreams.

CONTENTS

ACKNOWLEDGMENTS

A special thank you to my daughter **Jenny** for guiding me through the process of writing this book.

Sharon Kizziah-Holmes, thank you for your expertise and your publishing support.

THE BEGINNING

Every story has a beginning. I will start with the place where things that were not normal, ordinary things began to happen.

I grew up in the small town of Titusville, New Jersey. Titusville and Washington's Crossing were somewhat the same place. In the old days, there were about five hundred people living there and both places used the same post office.

River Drive was the one main street in town. Houses were on the east side of the street and the Delaware River on the west. The old steam locomotives ran through our back yards and the Delaware Raritan Canal was just east of the railroad tracks.

We were surrounded by water.

One other note of interest, when George Washington crossed the Delaware to attack Trenton on December 26, 1776, his route took him right in front of the house I grew up in.

FIRST FISH

My grandfather, uncle, and dad liked to fish. They caught catfish, bass, chain pickerel, walleyes, sunfish, white perch, eels, and occasionally big old snapping turtles. The local bar at the Crossing would give ya five bucks for a big turtle. They made turtle soup out of them.

These three fishermen would gather at Grand Pop's, cross over the railroad tracks, set their lawn chairs by the canal, and fish all day on a Sunday afternoon.

I was about five years old when I had my first encounter with the magical fish. I stood next to the railroad tracks and my grandfather's outhouse. I kept yelling that I wanted to fish, too. They wanted me to stay off the tracks.

They finally gave in to the pesky kid and gave me a six-foot cane pole with about five feet of line, a cork, and a minnow. They thought that would keep me quiet and out of trouble until I pulled in an 8-inch sunfish. They put it in a bucket and thought I would play with it and they could continue to fish. Not so.

I asked for another minnow. A few minutes later they heard an odd sound. Uncle Gobe yelled, "Grab him!" Dad grabbed me, my uncle grabbed my hands and the pole. I had hooked the "big one" and was waist-deep in the Delaware Raritan canal when I was rescued.

My 22-inch largemouth bass was the biggest fish of the day.

THE BIG FLOOD

I think it was around 1955 when we had the great flood. The Delaware rose 33 feet by our house. The flood caused significant damage to some homes on the north side of town, including taking a barn down the river and crashing it into the Washington's Crossing Bridge.

Everyone's big fear was that we could lose the town if the canal and river came together. Our family and most others were feverously loading sandbags and placing them on the railroad tracks to keep the two bodies of water from merging.

I was about nine years old and was told to stay off the tracks. They didn't need the kid there to slow them down.

Grand Pop said, "Why don't you see if you can catch some fish?" He said I could sit on his back porch and fish in his garden. I had some worms and there was plenty of water there, so I took him up on his offer.

Late that afternoon, when they had finished, they waded up to the porch and said, "Did you have any luck?" I said it was hard fishing but I didn't get skunked. They looked into my 5-gallon bucket and saw three big silver shiners and two small catfish. They shook their heads and went about getting dinner ready for all the workers.

Dad told my uncle that I had no concept of NOT catching fish. He said, "I think he talks to them." Thus, a Fish Whisperer was born.

SMOKING, THE BEGINNING
OF THE END

I think I was about nine or ten. My dad smoked, so I thought I would see what was so neat about puffing out smoke. I borrowed three of Dad's cigarettes and met up with some friends in the tunnel between the graveyards at the Presbyterian Church. Problem: four kids and three smokes.

I gave the cigarettes to my friends and I took an old hollow dead twig of some kind. We got them lit and made smoke. I got smoke and some hot ashes. Not a great experience.

It got worse when I got home.

Mom said she smelled smoke????? She said, "Were you smoking?" You did not lie to Mom or Dad. If you did, you were doomed. I said yes and confessed. She said she would not tell Dad if I promised to never smoke again. I promised.

Well, that should have been the end of a close call, with one exception. A few months later, two fifteen-year-olds were having a smoking contest in an old shack at the north end of town. I wasn't smoking, but there were three of us youngsters holding lit cigarettes.

The goal was to see how many cigarettes these two older guys could smoke at one time. A friend of mine, who had recently caught her hair on fire a few weeks ago, had just gone home. Her Mom saw smoke coming out of the old shack. My friend said all the guys were up there smoking. Her mom called my mom. The building only had three sides and no roof. I saw my mom going by the window. I jumped out the back of the building, crossed the creek on a log, and ran up the hill toward my house.

There she was at the top of the hill, with the dreaded big black belt. I felt that belt all the way home. Every time I said I wasn't smoking I got whacked. This was my one and only encounter with the big black belt. I think I finally convinced Mom that I was sorta telling the truth by the time I turned forty.

The only other time I saw the Big Belt in use was when my brother Donald did something that ticked off Mom. I think he cussed or something. Dad went after Donald with the belt. Donald's twin sister Dawn jumped on Dad to save her brother. She ended up being the one who got spanked.

THE CUB SCOUT INCIDENT

Yes, I was a Cub Scout. I survived in this great program for two years before fate did me in. I was a nice, polite little kid. My den leader was nice, but her son was a pain in the ASS.

We made crystals with coal and something on it that caused crystals to grow. Mine was beautiful. The little jerk picked my crystal up and said it was his. When I said, no, he couldn't have it, he dumped it on the floor and yelled loudly so his mother would come to his rescue.

I got even. A few weeks later, we were taking a den hike in Washington's Crossing Sate Park. We started about 9:30 in the morning. We all had our walking sticks and our emergency rope. The rope was just a 10-foot piece of clothesline. We were in a line with our den leader leading the way. I was next-to-last, with The Jerk just behind me.

There it was, mostly covered by leaves—a brand new hunting arrow. It was in perfect condition.

The Jerk said if I didn't give it to him he would tell his mom that it was his and that I stole it. I said I would give it to him if he could tie me to a tree and I couldn't get loose.

He laughed and said, "Ok." I, in turn, told him on a double dare that if I tied him up he would never get loose. Oh, yeah! Long and short, the story goes this way: I tied him to the tree using his rope.

Then I used my rope. Next, I said, "If you want this old arrow, you can have it." I chucked the beautiful hunting arrow into the tree just above his head. He cussed at me. I ran down the trail and caught up with the rest of the hikers.

It was about 6 pm that evening when my Mom received a call from his mom. She couldn't find her son The Jerk. Woops. I told mom he might still be in the park. Needless to say, things went downhill fast. We found him still tied to the tree. For some reason, his mom—my den leader— kicked me out of the den.

I might also mention that they had a dog, a nasty little Scottish terrier. He must have taken after The Jerk. A few months after the park incident, I rode my bike down the street by their house. The dog came after me. As he grabbed my pants, I lost the top of my chocolate ice cream cone. It hit him in the face. What a mess. He yelped, let go of my pants, and ran yelping all the way home. He never bothered me again.

A few months later, I started going to Boy Scout meetings. Troop 1776 held troop meetings at the Titusville Elementary School. I was at a patrol meeting at one Scout's house where we played some form of hide and seek.

It was dark, no moon, and while running full speed through the woods, I fell into a huge hole where they were building a new house. By the time I recovered, everyone else was gone.

A couple of weeks later, we were supposed to have another troop meeting at the elementary school. About 30 Scouts showed, up but the sign on the door said the meeting was cancelled due to no adult leadership. That was my last piece of youth Scouting.

I started seriously fishing again.

My one regret is that a few months later the troop reorganized and I didn't go. Their first trip was a week-long canoe trip on the Delaware River from upper New York state to Titusville. I guess it was about a 150-mile trip.

A BIG STEP FORWARD

By the time I was twelve, I was fishing every chance I could get. My first reel was an old Spin Joy with plastic gears. I told Dad and Uncle Gobe that the big fish would melt the gears.

Two days later, I hooked a huge carp in the old canal. The monster ran upstream toward the bridge. The drag squealed, locked up, and my line snapped. It sounded like a .22 rifle going off. My dad replaced the broken reel with a second Spin Joy. It only lasted about a week before another big carp did it in. Lo and behold, a few days later my dad and uncle presented me with my first reel with metal gears.

A few short weeks after getting a decent rod and reel, I had another life-changing experience. My uncle asked me if I would like to go with him to Silver Lake in North Jersey for the opening day of the TROUT season. The answer: "YES!"

It was strange, because it was cold and even snowed about an inch the night before. We were bundled up with gobs of clothing to keep warm. Our row boat drifted back and forth across the east side of the lake.

We were using night crawlers, two hooks, and split shot. After a couple of hours of freezing our butts off, I felt something and then didn't. A few seconds later, there was a definite tug. I pulled, set the hook, and caught my first trout.

The joke is, I caught two trout, one on each hook. A pair of 10-inch brookies were my catch of the day. My uncle ended up catching his limit, a combination of brookies and rainbows in that 8- to 11-inch range.

The day ended with my uncle hanging a 10-inch rainbow on a piece of monofilament line from a tree. He stood behind it and I took his picture. It made his fish look like it was as long as a yard stick. It was fun.

Later that year, I had the experience that hooked me forever on trout fishing. I had been told that there were trout being stocked in Stony Brook near Pennington, New Jersey. It was only about five or six miles from my house.

Mom and Dad took me over on a Sunday afternoon. I caught some sunfish, a couple of smallmouth bass, and a few creek chub minnows. There was an old, ragged-looking pine tree hanging over the creek, with a section of fast rapids gushing into the bank forming a deep, sunlit pool under the old tree.

The afternoon sun's rays beamed through the trees into the water. It lit up the bottom of the stream, showing every pebble, rock, twig, and the green moss that covered some of the larger rocks. Three casts in a row, something shot out from under the tree and whacked my night crawler. Each time, my bait was gone and I didn't get the fish.

Then I saw it. It was absolutely the most gorgeous fish I had ever seen. Its fins were jet black, bright red, and milky white. The underbelly and sides were a mix of crimson and gold. Its dark blue-green back was full of light-colored, irregular lines running through it.

Blue and red spots added to the other markings that made this brook trout so beautiful as it held its own in the sunlit rapids under the old tree. It was in its spawning colors. I didn't catch this one, but it left a beautiful visual memory that would last a lifetime.

THE TEACHER

I didn't realize we were sort of poor in the old days. We lived with my Great Grand Mom Most. I remember running through the snow to the outhouse in the back yard, and the first day we had indoor plumbing.

Dad worked six days a week as the meat cutter at the Food Mart in Princeton. He rode the bus 16 miles one way each day before we got our first car. After we got a car, Dad took us to the Hunterdon County Drive-In theatre every Saturday night during the summer.

It was $1 a car-load. My favorite night was a dusk-to-dawn John Wayne night. We saw The *Searchers*, *Fort Apache*, *The Horse Soldiers*, *Rio Grande*, and *The High and The Mighty*. Mom and Dad were great parents. I don't ever remember feeling anything but loved and cared for.

My Uncle Gobe, on the other hand, was single, had a good paying job, and sort of adopted me. He became my fishing teacher and something of a second father.

Uncle Gobe's real first name was Grover. I called him Go Go when I was little, then Gobe as I got older. By the time I was twelve, everyone called him Gobe.

I would go to his house every Friday night during trout season. We would get up at 3 am, stop at the Flemington Diner at 3:45 for breakfast, and be fishing the Musconetcong River by 5 am. We would both have our fish limit before noon and would stop by Mom's Diner on the way home. You could get a monster sausage, onion, and pepper sandwich with a milkshake for $1.50.

We also fished the Mohakaway, Pittstown Creek, Pequest, Big and Little Flat Brook, Spruce Run, Paulinskill, and the South Branch of the Raritan River.

I kept a fish record from 1958 to 1964. I didn't keep all the trout I caught, but kept the record to try and show improvement in numbers, size, and location of fish caught. The numbers went this way: 12, 23, 48, 120, 187, 248, 320.

I gravitated to a small Colorado single-hook spinner during my teenage years. By the time I was a junior in high school, I was out-fishing my uncle in numbers, but he always caught the big one.

One more thought: most of the trout caught in my youth were in that 8- to 12-inch range. There were a few 16-inchers. I did catch a 21-inch brown in a fishpond at the County Fair, but that one doesn't count.

GIRLS

I didn't have a girlfriend when I was in high school, but that doesn't mean I didn't like them. I will loosely provide an explanation without mentioning names.

One girl I played with could hit a softball ball further than any of us guys. She was good. She would hit the softball into the Delaware Raritan Canal and walk around the bases while we tried to fish the ball out of the water.

There was another young lady I had an interest in. I had her brother teach me how to play bridge. I thought this would be a way to build a relationship with her, but I don't remember her ever playing cards with us. At least it got me in her house. I used to ride my bike down the sidewalk and through the alley in an effort to see her and just say hello.

I also made a special effort to be nice to another girl one Christmas. We drew names at our church youth fellowship meeting one Sunday. I drew her name.

What can you get a nice girl for Christmas that she would always remember? I had a great idea. She smiled as she began to unwrap her present. The expression on her face changed significantly and she almost dropped the glass cage housing the two cute white mice. She politely said thank you and took them home that night.

Two weeks later she called me and asked if I could take them back. It seems they got loose in the kitchen and her mom found one on the kitchen counter top. The mouse saga ends several months later when my two supposedly MALE mice had a slug of babies.

My younger brother was playing with the mice and forgot to close the cage door and they all escaped. For weeks you could hear them running through the walls in our house. Then all went silent. ?????? I still think the mouse gift was a good idea. I feel bad for the mice.

Note: According to an innocent bystander, one local young lady made the comment that there were no eligible boys in Titusville. I guess that's why I spent most of my time fishing. Considering where and how I ended up, I think she was wrong.

EIGHTH GRADE

I can only remember three things when it comes to junior high or middle school.

First, there was a history teacher who went out of her way to get me to recite the Gettysburg Address. She let me do it two lines at a time. It took weeks to get it done. When it came to memorizing stuff like that, I just froze.

I also remember the lady in charge of the spring concert. She kicked me out of the choir two days before the show because I was throwing off three rows. My voice was changing. She could have left me in and just told me to mouth it. It would have been less embarrassing.

My most memorable incident came on a trip to the boys' room. You see, there were three floors to this old red brick school building. I think the boys' room was on the north end of the building on the first and third floor. It was located on the south end on the middle floor. It's a little confusing.

I walked in and sat down. Someone else came in and sat down in the stall right next to me.

When I saw the skirt drop to the floor, I knew I was in big trouble. I waited till she left and made a beeline for the door. As I came out, another girl was coming in.

I can still see the smile and frown on her face as we passed. She never told anyone about my moment of stupidity. She just shook her head and smiled. She was an ACE.

LEMMING'S CREEK AND SWIFT'S WOODS

We called this little creek Lemming's Creek because it ran by Lemming's Gas Station. Shad and herring moved up the creek a short way from the Delaware in the spring. The only natural year-round fish were minnows and pumpkinseed sunfish.

My Aunt Mary lived about a mile upstream and had a very small spring on her farm. We caught stocked trout in the canal and planted them in the creek. That effort failed when a youngster up on the hill caught them and took them home. He left them on the porch overnight and his mom planted them under her tomato plants the next morning. What a waste.

Some friends and I used this area for one of our great experiments. We cut some trees down in Swift's Woods along the creek and proceeded to turn them into logs with notches in them, like Lincoln Logs.

We were building a real log cabin. We used pulleys and a horse to move logs into position. We were ready to put the roof on when we got hit. Someone with crow bars tore apart some of the logs while we were in Sunday school.

This happened twice before we got smart. We skipped Sunday school and waited. Some guys our age from up on the hill showed up and started to pull things apart. We attacked. Without going into any details, we won the battle and finished the cabin. We used large spike nails through the notches in the logs to make sure no one would find it easy to mess up our masterpiece.

THE GARBAGE LADY

O nce a month, the Garbage Lady would show up at Grand Pop's in a big black car driven by her chauffeur. He always wore a suit and tie with dark sunglasses. She owned the trash company and personally came by to collect her money. She was a super-kind old gal who, for some reason, looked forward to meeting this young teenager as she came through town.

When the car pulled up and the back passenger-side window came down, she would yell, "Hey, boy, ya have anything special for me today?"

She carried a large ice chest in the trunk of the limo in hopes I had some channel or blue catfish for her.

I fished the Delaware hard the two days before she made her rounds and kept my catch alive in Grand Pop's old wash tub under the faucet by the back porch. She didn't want dead stuff, just fresh live ones.

She paid me 75 cents to a dollar for most fish. She gave me $3 for the big cats. Once, I had a 3-foot-long monster eel as big around as my arm. She gave me a $5 bill for that critter. When you get 50 cents an hour for mowing lawns, the $10 to $15 a month from the Garbage Lady seemed like a fortune. I was getting paid to fish.

There is one other thing I feel I need to say. I think the five hundred people who lived in Titusville when I was a kid were all white. This kind lady from Trenton was black. She holds a special place in my memory and made a positive difference in the life of a teenage boy.

THE BIRD OF PARADISE

S ometimes we remember the little things that left a memory somewhere deep in our sub-conscience. Someone says something that switches on that little button and up pops a long-stored piece of our past. It was filling out a Christmas card for my cousin in New Jersey that released this thought.

We got together at my cousin's house on Friday nights one year to watch Friday Night at the Movies. His family had the first color TV in our town that I know of.

It was *The Bird of Paradise*, starring Debra Paget, Louis Jourdan, and Jeff Chandler, that left a significant teenage memory. It was a love story, a little sexy, and had a tragic ending. Debra Paget jumped into the volcano to appease the gods and save her people. I was smitten and definitely moved by Debra Paget. I might also mention my cousin was and still is a super-nice guy.

CAMPING WITH DAVID

D ave was my best friend. Before we had cars, Dave's dad provided transportation to a number of creeks and lakes.

One such trip was to the South Branch of the Raritan River. This was a fly-fishing-only stream with lots of big rocks and fast water. Dave's dad dropped us off and would come back the next day to pick us up.

We set up our tent on a small island and started to fish. I had the right fly and hooked lots of fish, but they kept getting off. This was bad, because we had planned on eating fish for dinner.

The only provisions we had were some matches, tin foil, and a can of tuna fish. I have no idea why we had the tuna fish.

Late that afternoon, I finally got lucky and hooked a 14-inch brown trout. He flipped off and landed on a gravel bar. I grabbed him before he could jump back into the river. It was then I noticed I was fishing with a fly with half of the hook broken off. I believe I broke the hook early that morning when I snagged a tree on my back cast.

It was not the best meal, but when you are hungry, you do the best you can. We stuffed our trout with tuna fish, wrapped it in tin foil, dropped it in the hot coals, and ate a light supper. I learned to check hooks, especially after getting caught in trees.

THE GREAT SMOKY
MOUNTAINS TRIP

It was mid-summer when my best friend Dave called to ask if I would like to go fishing in the Great Smoky Mountains in North Carolina. He, his dad, and older brother thought I would be a good companion for Dave. My answer was a definite YES. I think we were in our early teens at the time and this was a big deal.

We were on the Blue Ridge Parkway and ended up camping in the national park just outside the town of Cherokee, North Carolina.

On our first full day, Dave and I fished in the park. It was a small, very cold mountain stream and we didn't have any waders. Using a spinner, we caught a few very small rainbows in that 4- to 6-inch range.

Late that afternoon, we went to Cherokee to get some food items. It was on this little run that we hit pay dirt. While Dave's dad and brother shopped, we started casting night crawlers.

This was a big river and we could see fish breaking on the surface. We ended up with enough nice rainbows to feed the four of us for dinner. Late that evening, after a short shower, we started catching night crawlers for the next day.

That's when things went south.

The park ranger came by and asked us what we were doing. We told him we were catching worms. He said, "You can't use them in the park." We said we knew that. He said the Indians in the town of Cherokee were looking for people who were fishing without an Indian permit on a stocking day. Whoops! I wondered why everyone was watching us.

Two hours later, a bear came into camp and gave us a hard time. I think he smelled the fish.

It was at that point that we packed up and moved out. I think we were trying to avoid a potential serious problem.

Our trip was shortened, but we did find one gem of an item to take home. We came across a fireworks stand and bought a bunch of incher firecrackers. I think we paid $2.50 for a package containing 2500. (These fireworks show up in another spot in my memoirs.)

When it comes to permits and rules, we had screwed up. But we learned our lesson and never repeated that error again.

THE DELAWARE MONSTERS

The Delaware River had, and still has, its secrets. There are those fish that we never saw, never landed, but let us experience the strength of those fish that were way too big and strong for us early teenaged kids to mess with.

The story starts with a trip up Lemming's Creek to catch a bucketful of large creek chub minnows. The best ones ran in that 6- to 8-inch range. From there, we would go down to Mr. Smith's dock.

We were ready to battle the monsters. We had a big net, Grand Pop's old casting rod and reel with a double-hook setup, and 50-pound test line. We thought we were invincible. The fish we landed were mostly big, but not the monsters. We caught catfish up to 10 pounds, a 36-inch monster eel, and an 8-pound largemouth bass one night. It was the fish that left us confused and defeated that made these nighttime adventures a big deal.

A good example of our frustration occurred on a moonless night in the early 60s. Our poles were tied to the dock with clothesline to keep them from being jerked into the river. We sat there with our kerosene lantern waiting for that one big strike.

Then it came. One short sharp jerk, the pole bent slightly as the old casting reel squeaked. The line went slack and rolled back toward the dock and slowly started moving out and up the river. It was time. I set the hook, and the pole bent as far as it could go without breaking.

The old drag on the reel was set tight, but the line still went out. The monster slowly swam upstream nonstop for over 50 yards. It was like it didn't even realize that it was hooked. At about 70 yards, the line went limp and the one-sided struggle was over. The line held, but he straightened out the hook.

As I look back on those early days, we must have been defeated at least half a dozen times. As an adult, I can only think of a handful of potential monsters of the deep that existed back then and perhaps run the Delaware to this day. Huge catfish over 50 pounds, sturgeon coming up from the ocean, and humongous stripers in that 40- to 50-pound range could have been our monsters of the Delaware.

THE COVE

T he Cove was a long, boulder-strewn piece of land that jutted out into the Delaware about a half-mile up the backroad north of Titusville.

The water was fast and deep on the west side of the Cove, and calm and deep on the east side. It was here, one spring just after the ice went out, that we spotted a huge snapping turtle about six feet down in the mud. I think it was sorta hibernating.

My best friend and I used a treble hook to try and snag this critter. After several failed attempts, we got lucky and managed to drag it up onto a sandy gravel area. I think it was still half-asleep. We tried to carefully carry or drag it to Grand Pop's.

As the snapper woke up, it was obvious we needed a new strategy if we were to succeed in getting this 20-pounder to the old wash tub.

We used our walking stick, an old broom handle. We each held an end and moved the middle of the broom handle in front of the turtle's nose.

He got mad, clamped down on it, and held on until we made it to the old wash tub. That's when he really got mad and snapped the stick in two.

This story ends with the snapper becoming turtle soup at the bar in Washington's Crossing. The five dollars we got for the turtle was equal to ten hours of lawn-mowing wages. That was a big deal back in the 60s.

MY SECRET PLACE

There is one small spring-fed brook in New Jersey that I call my Secret Place. Tall pine trees, huge boulders, small waterfalls, and crystal-clear water make up this sanctuary of heavenly fishing.

You had to crawl on your hands and knees to sneak up on these wild, spooky fish. In the early days, you caught a few rainbows and browns in the lower reaches, and native brook trout in the headwaters. This has always been a catch-and-release stream for me.

It was a heavenly place. In 1964, just before going into the US Air Force, I set my one-day teenage record on this little creek. In eight hours, I caught and released 98 trout.

Nowadays, I believe most people ignore this little creek, but I still come back every few years to give it try. It is now a totally wild trout stream with a few native browns and lots of brook trout.

A few years ago, she gave me a real surprise. I caught 5 tiger trout out of two small pools below a little waterfall. I guess a brookie and brown decided they were isolated in this stretch of water and said, "You look good to me," and away they went.

SELF DEFENSE

O ne thing I was really good at during my early teens was throwing rocks.

I was tall and skinny. Older kids made fun of me and gave me a hard time.

They tied me to a telephone pole next to the railroad tracks. I was there for hours before getting loose. If you have to pee, that's a serious problem.

Some guys threw rocks in the canal when I was fishing to scare my fish.

I found out that the big pieces of granite on the track beds made a good self-defense option. It was whack-em-with-a-rock or run. I ended up doing both.

The last use of this defense option occurred behind my house while fishing in the canal.

An unnamed individual threw some rocks in the canal. I gave my traditional warning, with a piece of granite in my hand. He stopped pitching rocks and walked on by.

When he thought he was safe, he grabbed some stones and threw them at my cork. He ran a few yards, crossed the canal bridge, and was running home along the road.

I let fly a piece of granite as he moved between the trees on the other side of the canal. Whack!

Eight stitches and a visit from the local powers that be brought my rock-throwing career to an end.

STUPID DANGEROUS THINGS

L ooking back, I realize that we all did some things as kids that we should have avoided, things we don't want our kids or grandkids to do. We were not bad. We were just experimenting and having fun.

For example: firecrackers.

They were illegal in New Jersey, but you could get some small ones across the Delaware in Pennsylvania. I had a friend who got some bigger stuff from another state. And if you got to the Titusville Elementary School at daybreak the morning after the Fourth of July fireworks display— the cleanup crews didn't arrive until eight or nine—you could find super-neat stuff that had failed to explode.

FIRECRACKERS #1: THE BATTLESHIP

One time, we took a bunch of differently sized and shaped cardboard boxes and taped them together in the form of a battleship. Our ship was about 10 feet long and had a silhouette in the moonlight that showed her big guns and conning towers.

She was filled with paper and about 10 packs of incher firecrackers, about 20 firecrackers per pack. Three cherry bombs were located in the center third of our masterpiece.

We launched her in the moonlight from a motorboat in the middle of the Delaware a little after 10 pm. It was beautiful.

We set her afire and the wind literally pushed her up the river. From a distance, we watched her burn with intermittent explosions. She sailed for about 10 to 15 minutes before the cherry bombs tore her apart. Split in two, she slowly burned, exploded, and went down in flames.

FIRECRACKERS #2: HALLOWEEN

E ach Halloween, we would go out the night before trick-or-treat night and throw corn kernels on porches and soap widows. You did it and ran. Sometimes people would throw water balloons at you in retaliation. It was fun and no one got hurt.

One year, we discovered a new tactic. This one was not so good, even though we thought it was fun at the time. We found that you could take a plastic pick-up stick and tape it to a porch railing. Next, a pack of incher firecrackers would be pushed up against the railing through the pick-up stick.

We would take a match, light the plastic pick-up stick, and run. We would be two blocks away before the explosions. Our local police force would show up, but we were already gone.

That worked out well until we got to the lumber yard and set off some random fireworks there and behind a church. Two police cars—one coming from the north, the other from the south, while we were behind the Presbyterian Church—put us in a bind.

We had the canal on the east and the river on the west. We were trapped. There were four or five of us in the group.

Everyone but me hid in the graveyard. I ran like hell through backyards and leaped over fences until I reached my house. I ran inside, told my mom about the fireworks, etc., put pajamas on, grabbed a glass of milk, and sat down in front of the TV.

When the doorbell rang, Ray, a local police officer who went to high school with my mom, asked if I was in. My mom pointed to me sitting in front of the TV.

He laughed, shook his head, and said, "Don't let him go back out tonight." He left. I was safe.

All of my friends were caught hiding in the graveyard. They were taken to the police station where they were picked up by their parents and had to give up their firecrackers.

I was lucky. I still had my firecrackers. My mom and dad said that was enough. No more trick-or-treating for me.

FIRECRACKERS #3: THE BIG STUFF

O ur firecracker thing went even further than the ship or Halloween. We used the big stuff from the Fourth of July celebration to see if we could blow up a huge old dead tree down on the edge of Washington's Crossing State Park.

We drew straws to see who would get the opportunity to light the extremely-short fuse on this eight-inch thing we found at the elementary school after the Fourth. I'm glad I failed to draw the short straw. My best friend won the draw.

He used a punk to light the fuse. There was a spark, then nothing, and then a spark, a bright flash, and dirt and tree flying in all directions. My friend was dazed and had black soot all over him.

Once again, we ran like hell as the monster old dead tree came crashing to the ground. It made a huge cracking sound on the way down. I think it was on fire.

I will just mention two other items without the details.

The first is building a mortar launcher that shot a D battery clean across the Delaware river. Don't do this during the Fourth of July boat race. It becomes a no-win situation.

The other thing occurred during a late-summer heat wave. The river was extremely low. Catfish and suckers were dying. We suspect this was caused by low oxygen or pollution of some kind.

We discovered that silver tubes somehow would burn under water. We used them to put some fish out of their misery. Once again, I will skip the details.

I might also mention that the Delaware is much cleaner nowadays. There is some great smallmouth, walleye, and channel cat fishing around Titusville. We also have stripers and shad coming up from the ocean to spawn.

THE KING PIGEON

My grandfather worked at the County Work House. He ran the stone crusher and supervised a number of low level convicts.

There were lots of pigeons there. He brought a few young squabs home and gave them to me to raise. I built a really nice three-level pigeon coop that comfortably housed about a dozen birds.

A big old wharf rat moved in from the old canal one night and killed one of my smaller birds. I decided, for their safety, to leave the pen open so they could get out if stressed.

A few days passed before the rat returned looking for another easy meal. When I went out to feed my birds that morning, all the pigeons except my King Pigeon were gone. The rat was dead in the bottom of the cage and the King, though injured, stood proudly on his perch.

This story has an interesting, somewhat funny end. My mom became a deacon in the Presbyterian Church. She came home from a church meeting and said it was going to cost the church a small fortune to clean the pigeon poop out of the church steeple.

She looked at me, smiled, shook her head, and started cooking dinner. They were my pigeons. I could make a cooing sound, hold my hand out, and the King and his girlfriend would come down from the steeple and land on my arm.

WILD CAT HAIRY

I bring up Wild Cat Hairy at this time because my stories about him started about the time I went into the Air Force and continue to this day.

I used to tell the adventures of this creature after dark in the Titusville Presbyterian Church graveyard, around lonely campfires, or in any other suitably spooky place that was available. Such settings were a necessary part of the atmosphere. No Wild Cat Hairy tale was complete without dramatic narration, expressions, gestures, and sound effects—especially Hairy's iconic roar, which my kids (and grandkids, nieces, nephews, and innumerable other once-youngsters who huddled together in the shadows with me) still remember.

Hairy was a superhero. He minded his own business but came to the aid of any creature that needed him.

The original story starts like this.

Millions of years ago, the sky was full of smoke and fire. Volcanoes were spewing red-hot lava and lightning flashed across the sky. There were large and small creatures on the Earth. It was a rough place to live or just survive in.

There was a great tree growing out of a massive boulder on the side of a rocky mountain. A flash of lightning struck the tree. It exploded and the boulder below split in two.

Out of the fire and smoke, he came. The creature was small and moved silently through the night. His eyes glowed laser-red and his claws were razor sharp. He jumped up on a huge boulder, surveyed his kingdom for the first time, and let out a screeching roar.

Thus was the birth of a superhero, Wild Cat Hairy.

UFOS

I have encountered unidentified flying objects twice so far in this lifetime.

I was in my early teens, sitting on Grand Pop's dock, fishing with big creek chub minnows for the monsters we knew lived in the Delaware.

The old casting rod had 50-pound test line on it and I felt invincible. Suddenly, the line went slack and then slowly began to move up river. I set the hook and the fight was on. The battle was short-lived. The unknown monster went 50 yards upriver nonstop, when my line went limp.

The line held, but he straightened out my hook.

That's when it happened.

A bright circular light glided silently over the treetops in Pennsylvania, made its way out over the river, turned around, and went back to Pennsylvania. This silent thing made 26 identical trips over the next hour.

By the time its mission was completed, most everyone in Titusville saw it. On its last circular trip, it stopped over the middle of the river. It dropped a bright light on the water, like a flashlight held upside-down.

The light went out and the sphere moved west for the last time.

Grand Pop witnessed this event sitting in his rocking chair on his front porch with his 12-gauge shotgun in his lap. He was ready for the invasion that didn't come.

The media said it was a military glider taking pictures on a practice mission. The retraction of this statement came several days later, saying the glider mission was downriver south of Philadelphia.

The second UFO event happened while I was in the Air Force and stationed on Okinawa. Although things are a little foggy, I think it went this way.

My roommate worked radar and I was in communications. He watched things happen on the radar screen and I sent messages to other military installations.

We had recently lost an aircraft that had been launched to check out a potential plane moving across the China Sea. The Chinese and the US tested each other's response times. This back-and-forth movement was normal until our plane disappeared without a trace.

The next UFO showed up several days later. The whole 51st Fighter Wing went up.

As our aircraft moved in formation through heavy cloud cover, they lost the radar signal. One plane on the far left of the formation picked up the signal and moved in. He fired his sidewinders and they appeared to go right through the UFO without detonating. Our pilot said something about a blinding flash of light and he was gone.

According to my roommate, the UFO left the radar screen at 4,000 miles per hour and still climbing.

I can tell this story because some idiot sold a copy of the message concerning this event to the Okinawa press for $25.

FOOD AND OTHER THINGS

At our house, if you put it on your plate, you were expected to eat it.

Mom put lima beans on my plate. I told her I didn't like them, they made me feel sick. She made me eat them. I got sick.

Lima beans and warm tomatoes were not my favorite things when I was a kid. All other things were doable. For example, my cousin and I, when we were seven or eight, decided to make a new type of sandwich.

We started with white bread, lots of butter, and added long strands of clean green grass. It was getting dark, so we lightened it up by catching some lightning bugs. We pushed them head-first into the butter between the blades of grass. It was pretty. I don't recommend this to anyone. Way too much butter.

Another food source I bailed out on came a few years later. An elderly man who lived next to my grandparents invited me into his house. He had some ancient fishing equipment he thought I could use.

I took the old lures but politely turned down his treats.

You see, he loved chocolate. In his fridge, he had frozen chocolate-covered night crawlers, crickets, grasshoppers, and ants. There might be lots of protein there, but I still politely declined. My excuse was that it was almost dinner time.

Last but not least, I might mention my son Ben's Boy Scout eating habits that came along some years down the road.

His patrol was cooking dinner one night.

They were having hot dogs and baked beans. They put the dogs on the end of sticks and burned them till they fell off into the coals. They said they were done when black and crusty on the outside and just a little pink in the middle.

They cut the lid on the can of baked beans halfway open, put the can in the fire, and said they were done when half of the beans boiled over and out of the can.

The adult leaders decided to cook their own food. Good decision.

SPORTS

I had a rough time with sports in the early days. In my first year of Little League, I only got to play right field in the last inning. I got to bat four times in my second year.

My Uncle Wuffy was the head Little League umpire. He said if I didn't swing the bat, he would call everything a strike. He said, "If you have to, close your eyes and swing." So that's what I did.

I swung at a curve ball with my eyes closed. It hit me in the arm. It's a heck of a tough way to reach first base.

Note: I was on a team that had not lost a game in two years. Winning was the only thing the coach cared about.

I tried out for the varsity basketball team as a junior. I couldn't run the length of the court without losing the ball. The coach said to practice over the summer and try again next year. I did.

In my senior year, about 50 people tried out for the team. The coach was only going to take 12 or 13 players. I was number 14. For some reason, I keep thinking I got beat out by a girl trying out for the guys team. ???

The following week, luck showed up. Due to my last name starting with an E, I was in the gym class that met at the end of the day and was full of all the jocks. We were playing four-on-four basketball and I played against the backup varsity center. I got the rebounds.

It turns out, if you are 6-foot-3 and can jump higher than anyone else in your class, you get a second chance. I wasn't great, but I did what was needed. I did a good job rebounding and scored 4 points in one game.

Last but not least, I played fast-pitch softball while in the Air Force. I started in right field, went to third base, and ended up being a pretty good pitcher.

They said I was sneaky fast. That means my pitches looked like a slow boat to China, but took a big hop at the end. I pitched for a number of years and then went to slow-pitch by the time I was in my mid-thirties.

My single biggest success came in Joplin, Missouri. I pitched for a church team in a city league. I discovered that if you swing hard and level, and send the ball up the middle, you end up with a great batting average.

I led the league that year with a 700 batting average. I hit the outfield fence several times but never hit one over the fence. Because we had some big farmboys in our league who hit lots of homeruns, they raised the fence from 6 to 12 feet. I hit the top of the new fence one time. Too bad they raised it when they did.

My First Car and the Flies

I ran a trapline in the winter of 1963 and 1964. Muskrats and raccoons made up the majority of what I caught. I remember one skunk that made life difficult, and a couple of opossums that played dead until I tried to release them.

I also remember falling through the ice on the Delaware one winter. It was deep and I had waders on. I was lucky. I caught a sturdy tree branch on the way down and pulled myself safely up and out of the frozen river. Had I missed the branch, it could have been the end of this young fish whisperer.

I used my trapping money to buy my first car. It was a 54 Chevy or a Ford, with a green roof and yellow body.

The joke is, I paid $198 for a ten-year-old car and then had to pay $212 for insurance. What a bummer.

I drove the car for a year before going into the USAF, and my dad drove it for three more until the engine fell out on the ground in the middle of Princeton.

Dad said it was a good old car for four years. It was worth the 10 bucks to have it towed to the junk yard.

I look back on my trapping days and feel a bit sad about all the critters I caught. I don't trap any more.

It was during this same period that I did something I thought was funny at the time, but now regret having done.

I had an economics class followed by a history class. The history teacher was tough and scary. No one messed around in his class. It was just the opposite in economics. It was terrible.

Whenever the old teacher turned his back to write on the blackboard, rubber bands and paperclips flew all over the place.

My part in this mess went this way. If you catch about ten big blowflies and tie different colored pieces of thread with a slip knot to their feet, you can have a blast.

I carried them in an old wooden match box and released them in the economics classroom. It was gorgeous to see all those different colored threads attached to my flies gliding all over the room.

The teacher just ignored all this stuff and did the best he could.

HOT DOG JOHNNY'S

The Pequest River in North Jersey flows westward into the Delaware. I have caught brookies and rainbows in the Pequest, but never really got to know her.

I believe there is a trout hatchery on the river and a very good catch-and-release fly section, both of which I never had the opportunity to visit. My one good memory of this stream covers the stretch of river just before it hits the Delaware.

It was one of those mornings. I sat on a large boulder between two pine trees as the morning sun shot through the fog. It was like being in church.

Actually, I skipped Sunday school. There went my perfect attendance. I blame it on my first car and the fact that I was about to go into the USAF. But watching the sun hit the water through the fog and treetops really was like being in church.

By noon, I had my limit of 8- to 10-inch brookies and one 14-inch rainbow. It was lunchtime. The only place open worth eating at was Hot Dog Johnny's.

Lunch consisted of two hot dogs, lots of onions, ketchup, and mustard, topped with a big pickle. You got to wash it down with a huge mug of root beer. It was a good morning.

My brother tells me Johnny's is still there.

SKUNKED

Just after getting my first car at age 17, I decided to try a new fishing spot. I don't remember the name of this stream in northwest New Jersey, but I do remember what happened.

I was up and fishing at daylight. It seemed like a nice creek with lots of water and rapids. The excitement went downhill rather fast. I tried everything from spinners, worms, to flies, but nothing seemed to work. By 10:00, I was back at the bridge.

An elderly gentleman came by in an old rusty truck and asked how I was doing. I told him I didn't even have a bite.

He laughed and said, "Do you see that foam at the bottom of the rapids?"

I said I did. He laughed again and said that two days ago, the sewage plant overflowed and killed everything in the creek.

I tell this little story because this is the only time I have ever gone fishing and gotten SKUNKED. And it wasn't my fault.

THE NEXT FOUR YEARS

After high school, I spent the next four years in the USAF. I went through basic training at Lackland Air Force Base in Texas.

It was hot and dry.

The food was OK, but you only had fifteen minutes to eat it.

I guess being a tall skinny 6-foot-3 country boy made me a target. Our drill sergeant gave me a hard time for bouncing when we marched. I didn't make my bed or tie my shoes the way he wanted it done, so he constantly put me on nighttime guard duty.

We had rules to follow while on guard duty. You didn't let anyone in your barracks until they showed you their ID.

As I walked down the hallway to my room at a guard change, I heard my young replacement yell, "Stop!" Someone had opened the door without the proper identification. I ran to the guard's rescue, hit the door like a defensive lineman, and broke the sergeant's arm. Not good.

The next day, I had to explain this incident to our Commander. That was the last I heard of it.

The day before graduation, my drill sergeant stopped us while marching and chewed me out again for bouncing.

He yelled, "Look at me when I'm talking to you!" He was much shorter than me. I looked down. He shook his head and cracked up. He smiled and said I was a hopeless case. Things got much better from that point on.

Over my time in the USAF, I was stationed in Texas, Okinawa, and Scott Air Force base in Illinois.

While at Kadena AFB on Okinawa, I took up painting landscapes along with fishing in the surf.

I caught fish there, but have no idea what kind of fish they were. It was both exciting and scary to run along the beach at night. The rolling waves just shimmered and glowed in the moonlight as thousands of jellyfish made their way through the waves, some washing up upon the beach.

One other thing I remember, my Okinawan friends collected sea urchins to eat. They said not to pick up the white sea urchins with black-tipped spines because they are poisonous.

I also found that when you only make $79 a month, it helps to have a second income. That extra $10-$12 a month from my hobby of landscape painting helped pay for my fishing.

THE BAR

I was only 19. Everyone said if you went downtown, you would catch the bug, etc. I never left the base except to fish during my first six months on the island of Okinawa.

On one of those fishing runs, I met an Okinawan girl who spoke English. She was the one who told me not to pick up the poisonous sea urchins. Her name was Sumiko. She worked as a bartender in one of the many bars in the town of Kadena. I ended up going there once a week.

Each night, I sat at the bar. I only bought one drink and talked to the girls when they weren't busy. The girls working there got guys to buy drinks. GIs tended to get plastered. The girls stayed sober.

On slow nights, I could dance with the girls and just visit. They taught me some Japanese and I taught them some English. We were just friends.

You know you have been accepted when you show up to the bar on your birthday and find a bag over the chair you normally sit in.

Seeing that, I sat in the next chair over, but when the mama-san (the boss lady) walked by, she pulled the bag off the other chair. The red-velvet back was embroidered in gold letters. It said "Deane san." It was my chair. They also gave a me a pen-and-pencil set on my birthday.

FATE

While on Okinawa, there was a call for volunteers to staff a communications center in Vietnam. They needed twelve communications specialists.

My name was second on the list.

The extra pay would more than double my monthly income. I was excited. It was at this time that the person in charge decided that they would not accept anyone under the rank of E-4. I only had two stripes, not three.

My name came off the list. What a bummer.

A few short months after the crew left for Vietnam, we received a message at our communications center saying that the entire group of volunteers had been killed.

Do you believe in fate? There have been several times in my life when, for some reason, I was spared.

BACK TO FISHING – 1

Shortly after getting to Scott AFB in Illinois, I found that Missouri had trout parks. There were four trout parks in the state. Each park had its own hatchery.

The lifeblood of each park started with a large 58-degree spring that produced great trout water. These spring creeks ran for a mile or so before running into bigger rivers.

My favorite was Meramec Springs.

I fished the trout park, but spent most of my time fishing the Meramec River below the park. There were lots of rainbow and brown trout for several miles downstream. An occasional 18- to 22-inch fish was the prize of the day.

Note: While in the Air Force, I spent my leave time going back to New Jersey to visit my family and my Secret Place. It consistently produced wild brook and brown trout. 35 to 40 trout would have made for an average day. An 11- to 12-inch fish was a big one. They were gorgeous!

SCHOOL

One of the best things our government ever produced was the GI Bill. I used it to help get a college education.

Belleville Area Junior College was my starting place. It was just outside of Scott AFB in the town of Belleville.

I worked on a history degree until a biology professor got me excited. It was the lab dissection of a cat's inner ear that pushed me over the edge.

He said anyone who could dissect the inner ear with NO cracks would get an A for the course. I had a weak B average at the time. Everyone in our class, including a straight-A student, failed to complete the task. It took my professor several minutes to find that itty bitty crack in my cat's inner ear.

He was confused when I showed up the next day and began to work.

He said, "What are you doing?"

I said, "My cat has two ears." He laughed. My second ear got me an A.

I transferred to SIU in Carbondale Illinois for my last two years. A degree in Zoology and a minor in Chemistry was the prize for four long, hard years of hard work. My emphasis was on Fish and Game Management.

A SHORT STORY

The following is a short story I put together in an English class while attending BAC in the late 1960s.

"The Great March"

It had been a long, hot, and foggy night in the rainforest. The ground was saturated, and the mud was ankle-deep as the troops prepared to move out that morning.

To lead a force of thousands takes a very special leader. The commander was big and strong. His instincts and decisions were based on experience. He had held his leadership position for a long time and no one would dare to challenge him.

The vegetation was tall and thick. At times, it blocked out the sun, turning the jungle into a ghostly place full of dark shadows as the troops moved out through the morning mist.

By mid-morning, the temperature passed 100 degrees. The heat and the rain were the least of their worries. One by one, soldiers were lost. The attacks came swiftly from the air. Others were lost quietly to snipers moving silently on the ground. Battered but undeterred, they marched on to the edge of the great barren wasteland.

The temperature reached 110 and the rocky ground shimmered in the heat as the commander gave the signal to move forward. Once again, they were under attack. The roar of the dark shadows and terrifying wind took a huge toll of life.

Nearly one third of the army's one hundred thousand souls had been lost. Once across the great divide, they settled into a large gully. The commander moved onto high ground and climbed a tall blade of grass to survey the territory they had crossed.

The birds from the air and the lizards and spiders on the ground were deadly, but the four-lane highway and its speeding cars and trucks proved to be a disaster to the army ants. The commander lowered his head as he came down from his lookout position. If he had seen the movie *Gone With The Wind*, he would have said, "Tomorrow is another day."

MORE GIRL INFO

I'm going to backtrack for a moment. When it came to dating, I was not the most successful dude. I may have been a danger to myself and others.

For example, a girl I dated for six months while in the service told me I was a really nice guy but not her type.

The next young lady had a horse. She wanted me to ride it.

She said, "It runs fast. If you want it to stop, just say whoa."

I said, "Whoa," and it stopped on a dime and threw me over its head, and I landed on my butt in a corn field.

While living in Shiloh just outside of Scott AFB, a roommate and I rented a house. I dated four girls in two years. All four ended up marrying my roommates.

It's hard to get a person to help pay the rent when you have a reputation like that.

I also wondered if having buck teeth had anything to do with my dates going elsewhere. You see, they sometimes get in the way when you're kissing someone.

STARTING A FAMILY

Perhaps the most important thing to come out of college was Mary. She was a student and worked in the library at BAC in Belleville.

I needed to find things, but had no idea how to use a library. Out of nowhere came Mary. She helped me find that first book. She was always there. I think she knew I needed help.

I took her to see a movie. We got lost in a torrential thunderstorm. I was going the wrong way on a one-way street. Somehow, we got turned around and made it to the show.

Mary was one of five children. I inherited a whole new family. We played ball and cards and went camping. There is no doubt in my mind that, she was my soulmate.

We dated for two years and spent our last two years of college at SIU married. She was a straight-A student and proofread most of my written work.

Our son Ben came along a year after we were married, and our daughter Jenny came along a couple of years later.

Back to fishing.

I taught Mary how to fish. We started with sunfish at a pond in Belleville, and she caught her first trout in Pittstown Creek in New Jersey.

We spent our honeymoon in Colorado in a pop-up camper that her cousin loaned to us as a wedding present.

It snowed on us almost every night while camping in Rocky Mountain National Park.

Coyotes howled at night, and there were lots of brook trout in the Big Thomson River where it ran through Beaver Meadow. Three beautiful cutthroat trout were caught on dry flies in a high mountain lake up on the Continental Divide.

We also shared our camper with some very noisy field mice that came in through the wheelwells each night.

If you want a scary experience, try camping out in September in the wilderness. Take an afternoon and evening to go into Estes Park for a shower, a good meal, and a movie. Then go back to the campground, where you are the only people, after watching the original *JAWS* movie.

Every sound wakes you up. I still see that guy chumming and the shark shooting up from down under. Big eyes and lots of teeth. Spooky. It was at that point that everything went flying, including the popcorn and the soda—what a mess.

NEW RELATIVES

When you find your soul mate, you also inherit her family. Mary had an older sister and three brothers. We played football, softball, and just had fun together.

There are two trips worth mentioning.

The first was a two-day campout next to a small lake in southern Illinois. We saw lots of animals and snakes in and around the lake.

My future brothers-in-law made fun of me when I set my sleeping bag up on a picnic table. I told them there were things in the night that I didn't want to have crawl into my sleeping bag. They laughed again as they laid their sleeping gear out on the ground.

I told them that around dark the whippoorwills would start calling. They would go all night unless something bad came around. It was about 3 am when the whippoorwills stopped on a dime.

I heard my fellow campers say, "Did you hear that?"

It didn't take them two minutes to end up on the picnic tables. I had the last laugh.

A canoe trip into the Boundary Waters Canoe Area in Minnesota was our next great adventure.

On our first day, we went from Belleville, Illinois, to Ely, Minnesota. We camped out in our cars in a park that night. Early the next morning, we drove about twenty miles down a dirt road. It ended at an old, broken-down, rusty bridge that once crossed a small river. We put our two canoes into the river, and the six of us began a ten-day trip into the wilderness.

We stopped on an island in a big lake to deal with a potential serious problem. My future brother-in-law couldn't see.

It was around 10 am when we decided to split up. Three would stay on the island, while Mike and I would take his brother Ed back to Ely. We made it to the medical clinic in Ely by mid-afternoon, and were fortunate to find out Ed had just left his contacts in for 48 hours or more. All would be ok.

What next?

Because it gets dark up North around 10:00 in the evening, we decided to try and canoe back to the island. It got dark while we were still on the river.

If you ever go down a remote river in the dark with the guy in front of the canoe holding a flashlight, and see red eyes following you, it's a bit scary.

It was a pack of wolves. I think we were just going in the same direction.

We hit the lake and could just barely see the flickering campfire on the island about a mile out into the lake. The fog quickly rolled in and it was pure luck that we made it back to the island.

The next day, we were making a long portage from one lake to another. We had two guys carrying each canoe, and two carrying packs, etc.

At the halfway point, we stopped at a break spot to get our wind and moan just a little. It was hot and the Minnesota state bird, the mosquito, was everywhere.

Suddenly, two people and one canoe came down the trail. One girl carried the packs and the other carried the 17-foot canoe all by herself.

As they passed by, the girl carrying the canoe yelled over to us, "If you guys need help, I'll come back and carry it for you...."

It's bad when one 115-pound girl out-does two big strong guys. Embarrassing.

Two days later, we were tired and hungry as we entered Lake Agnes. This lake was huge. In some places, we could not see the other side. The Canadian border ran east to west across the lake.

We had lots of bacon, pancake mix, maple syrup, corn meal, and a 10-pound bag of rice. Mike was in charge of food. I was supposed to supply the fish.

It was day five and we still had no fish.

The crew gave me a hard time and sent me out all by myself to solve the problem. I caught one 8-inch walleye and a small sunfish by 2:00 in the afternoon.

Then I got lucky. I had a minnow, split shot, with a cork and eight-pound test line. There was a huge explosion on the surface. My cork was gone. I set the hook, but came up empty. Everything looked fine. Even my minnow was alive. But, ah! There it was. My big red and white cork was full of holes. This made the light come on. I had an idea.

I paddled to shore and caught about a dozen frogs for bait. One was a monster frog to be saved for a frog leg dinner. I tossed the others one by one into the lily pads.

Over the next few hours I caught a limit of northern pike in that 28- to 32-inch range. I was down to my last frog when I got hung up on a big old log.

I was sliding the canoe in gently toward the log so as not to scare any fish when I saw it. A northern slowly went under my canoe moving out into the lake.

As I reached out to get my wounded frog off the log, I could still see the pike's tail on the log-side of the canoe. This had to be one of those 20-plus-pounders. Froggy was whooped. His swimming days were over. I had only one shot.

I pulled the monster frog out of the old coffee pot where he had been placed and put him on the hook. I tossed him by hand into the lake about 30 feet from my canoe.

He landed with a splash and immediately made several long strides through the water. On his fourth push, my frog-leg dinner disappeared. He was gone, sucked under in a swirl the size of a small boat.

My uncle taught me to be patient. I opened the bail on my real and watched the line slip off for about 20 feet. He stopped, then started slowly moving from this calm little bay toward the open lake.

I set the hook, but he just kept moving forward like he wasn't even hooked. I was in trouble. He was towing me and my canoe backwards out into the main lake.

The wind was up and waves were splashing against the canoe, and I was getting wet. This was scary, and I considered cutting my line, when he turned back into the calm little bay. He knew I was there now and made a flying leap and a mad dash forward, ripping off line from my drag. My line went limp, he was gone.

I figured he had snapped my eight-pound test line, but then I realized he had straightened out the hook instead. I thought this story had come to an end, when up popped Froggy. He was in bad shape. He pushed with one good leg. It propelled him in a slow moving circle that ended with another huge swirl. Froggy was gone. The big northern had finished his dinner.

It was close to 10 pm and getting dark when I made it back to our island camp. It seemed the rest of the crew was bent out of shape. They had been stuck on the island all day because all the canoe paddles were in my canoe. I think there would have been a hanging, but then they saw all the fish. We ate well that night.

AFTER GRADUATION

I thought I had put about 100 job applications in the mail a few weeks before graduation from SIU, but had zero replies or interest.

It turned out that I did the paperwork, my wife put the stamps on the envelopes, and then she put them in the glove compartment of the car for me to mail.

We found the un-mailed letters the day before graduation. This caused a quick trip to the unemployment office, where I was told I was over-qualified for the jobs they had at that time.

Two days later, I got a call from the old semi-bald guy from the un-employment office. He wanted me to meet someone who might be able to help me find employment.

It turned out the employment fella was a volunteer commissioner for the Boy Scouts. They offered me $50 to teach the Fishing merit badge at Pine Ridge Scout Reservation near Carbondale, Illinois.

I told them I could not pay the rent, etc. on $50 and take care of my wife and one-year-old. I ended up taking the job, but it went this way:

We went and stayed at camp. No rent, free food, and lots of fishing time. When the cook for the staff quit, they hired my wife Mary, giving her $150 to take the cooking job.

A couple days later, the Commissary Director wrapped his car around a telephone pole and broke his leg. They offered me another $150 to fill that position.

We ended up with $350, plus food and lodging, for the summer. It also led to what became my career. I'll cover that item a little later.

A HELPING HAND

If you are working 16 hours a day, ordering and processing food for 300 campers a week, it doesn't leave much time to teach the Fishing merit badge.

I told my students that if they had all the badge requirements completed, with the exception of catching three different kinds of fish, I would guarantee they would pass the course by meeting me at the dock at 5 am Thursday morning.

There was one young Scout that made my day, week, and summer. He was a short, heavy-set, very shy twelve-year-old. He asked if it was true he could earn the Fishing merit badge if he did all the requirement and showed up at the dock at 5 am.

I said "Scout's Honor, it's a guarantee."

I stumbled down the path to the dock about quarter to five. I noticed a blob on the dock. As I walked out on the catwalk, there he was. He was in his sleeping bag tied to the dock and attempting to undo the rope as I approached.

I asked, "What are you doing?"

He answered, "I didn't want to oversleep and miss my chance to earn this merit badge. It is the only one I might earn this summer, and I didn't want the other guys to make fun of me."

I provided the pole, a salmon-colored rooster tail spinner, and a rowboat, and took him to my secret place on the lake. It was a shady, tree-lined cove about four to six feet deep.

There was a rock-shale shelf near an old tree and some lily pads. It was set about 30 feet from shore with a significant drop-off at that point. We fished for an hour and a half.

His eyes lit up when he hooked that first fish. He had never fished before. A plump 12-inch smallmouth leaped out of the water and almost landed in the boat.

At the weekly Friday night campfire, my young fisherman received his Fishing merit badge. He also was presented a plaque stating that he was the fisherman of the week.

His burnt-engraved wooden award listed the 47 fish caught that morning in one and a half hours. Smallmouth, crappie, goggle eye, sunfish, and one 21-inch chain pickerel were all part of his victory. Three hundred Scouts and leaders gave him a standing ovation. What a great victory.

THE VAMPIRE MOUSE

A nother Pine Ridge Scout Reservation story worth telling is one that came close to having a bad ending. It starts with me putting food baskets together in the commissary.

The baskets went out to the camp sites where the Scouts would cook their own meals.

There he was. That little mouse was zipping across the commissary floor. He made one big mistake. He could not resist the cheese in the mousetrap.

Being a storyteller, I told some Scout that we needed to bury this mouse and do it in a special way. Somehow, the mouse was related to the bats flying around camp, and the bats had something to do with vampires.

We had a special burial ceremony in the woods that afternoon. The mouse was gently placed in a large match box with a tooth pick stuck in him. You know, vampires need a stake stuck in them.

The older Scouts made fun of the whole deal and I had a feeling they had some sort of plan to screw up the story.

Sure enough, they snuck back later that day and pulled the stake out of the mouse.

I went back that night and removed the mouse. The next morning the older Scouts, with younger ones following, dug up the box and freaked out when they the vampire mouse was gone. The whole camp was buzzing with, "Watch out for the bats," etc.

As everyone gathered for the Friday night campfire, I stood on a hill about fifty yards away on the west side of the lake. I wore a black cape, combed my hair back and held a flashlight under my chin. What a mistake.

Someone yelled, "Look, on the hill, it's the vampire!"

"Get him!" was the cry as hundreds of Scouts with stakes and hammers rose and began to chase me through the woods. Fortunately, I escaped the stakes.

The camp director let me know the next morning that there would be no more vampire stories. I said, "Yes, sir," and behaved the rest of the summer.

THE ALL-AMERICAN BOY

It was the week after camp closed that I had an encounter that would definitely determine my future. The camp director let Mary, Ben, and me stay at camp for a week as a thank you for giving him our efforts over the summer camping season.

I was told someone was going to drop by camp to meet me. I had on a holey t-shirt and old shorts with strings hanging on them and was barefooted when the big black limo pulled into camp. The passenger, dressed in a suit and tie, said he came to interview Dean Ertel.

I said, "Hello, I'm Dean."

He looked puzzled as we sat down at the picnic table and began to talk about filling out paperwork for potential employment with the Boy Scouts of America.

We visited for about 25 minutes, asking and answering questions about professional Scouting opportunities. His name was Jack Armstrong. I found out later that he held a high position with the BSA and that he was well-known by everyone but me. Jack Armstrong was the Wheaties All American Boy and an Olympic superstar athlete.

I spent the next two months after meeting Jack trying to sell Kirby vacuum cleaners. This sales job and living with my in-laws was not the best arrangement.

In October, I had an interview with the Boy Scout council in Columbia, Missouri, but did not get the job. I did manage to catch my brother-in-law's car on fire on the way home. The engine was in the back of the car and I could not figure out why everyone was waving, etc. at us as we drove through St. Louis.

Two days later, our old car was packed and we were about to leave for New Jersey, where we hoped I could find work, when the phone rang. Darwin Van Gorp, the Scout Executive of the Great Rivers Council in Columbia said he had another opening and it was mine if I wanted it. We said yes.

I spent the next 40 years working for the BSA. My positions and the communities I served gave me multiple opportunities to do some fantastic fishing.

The following is a list of towns and states we lived in: Eldon and Sedalia, Missouri; Faribault and St. Paul, Minnesota; Joplin, Missouri; Fargo, North Dakota; and

Springfield, Missouri. I had the opportunity to work with and for some fantastic volunteers and served over 220,000 youth over my 40-year career.

THE THANKSGIVING TURKEY

My first job with the BSA in 1972 covered five counties, with the Lake of the Ozarks sitting in the middle. We lived in Eldon, Missouri. I did a little trout and bass fishing, but mostly just worked.

In the beginning, I drove about 150 miles a day. I tried to cover four or five towns a day, attempting to meet and build a relationship with hundreds of volunteers. I was also responsible for raising the funds needed to keep our Scouting program moving.

It was a cool, damp September night around 11 somewhere near Lincoln, Missouri, when I was passed by a big truck full of cages. Suddenly, there was a huge white blob sailing toward my car. Thud, thud, thud, was the sound of a large white turkey bouncing along under my car.

I slowed and would have stopped, but a car behind me had stopped and some guy was chasing the turkey down the road. I moved on.

The next thing I remember, I was behind the turkey truck again. I found out that they put two turkeys in a cage. OOOOOPs, here comes number two. I stopped quickly, grabbed the old bird, and used some clothesline to tie it up. I thought, *Wow, I have a free Thanksgiving turkey*, as I tossed him in the back seat of the car.

You know your day is not going so good when the turkey escapes, flies over your seat, and tries to beat you to death with its wings while you're doing 60 miles-an-hour. The claws in my shoulder were also rather uncomfortable.

After a short but bitter struggle, he was recaptured, tied up tight, and placed in the trunk of the car. Yes, I had a turkey, but it wasn't free. The old bird had pooped all over the trunk and back seat of the car. What a mess.

ELDON AND SEDALIA, MISSOURI

L ake Taneycomo is a manmade lake that runs
through the town of Branson, Missouri. This is a
tailwater area that is heavily stocked with rainbow
and brown trout.

In the old days, when we lived in Eldon, Missouri, back in
the early seventies, you could easily catch your limit of
rainbows by noon. The fish grew fast and big by feeding
on a massive scud population. The fishing in this section
of the White River system is still good, but not what it
used to be.

My first boss would take four of us down to Taneycomo
in early March for a couple of days of serious fishing. We
rented boats and motored upriver for several miles, then
drifted down using salmon eggs in those days. It was cold
with a little snow at times, or it could be in the sixties.

I remember one trip that was fun and, to some extent,
funny.

By noon, we each needed one fish to fill our limits. We
didn't have anything under 15 inches.

We stopped on an island just upstream from the Fall Creek access area for lunch. I wandered over to the far side of the island to see if I could land one more big one.

I caught and released three twelve-inchers and let the other guys know I found a bunch of fish in a deep, dark rapids. One fella came with me. On my first cast, I hooked Mr. Big. It was deep and I couldn't get this monster into the net.

The gentleman with me took off his shoes, socks, and pants so he could wade into the pool and net my fish. He sat on a log for about ten minutes while I tried to tire out my fish. He finally waded into the freezing water, made some funny noises, and netted my fish.

The plus and the minus of this story goes this way: I ended up with a six-pound rainbow, and my friend with the net, who sat on the log in his jockey shorts, ended up with a massive case of chiggers in the last place you would ever want to have them.

LUCK

T here is bad and good luck when it comes to fishing. Sometimes, you can get both to occur on the same fishing experience. Once, back in the 1970s, I was on my way to Hohn Scout Reservation to help run the BSA program at the camp.

I stopped near the bridge in Gravois Mills, on the Lake of the Ozarks, just to take a couple of casts. I was using a floating plug that looked like a frog, when bad luck struck. The plug was hit by a 10-inch bass, I set the hook, and the line broke. Dang it. It was old line and I should have replaced it.

A few seconds passed and then a fish jumped. It was the little bass. On its third jump, it threw the plug. I quickly fished it out of the water with a long stick. Having not learned my lesson, I retied the plug and took a few casts on the other side of the bridge.

The explosion occurred on the second cast. A monster largemouth came flying out of the water, flipping the plug back and forth in its huge mouth, and landed on a large gravel bar with about an inch or two of water on it. The big bass was swimming in a wide circle on the bar when I jumped in and ran through knee- to waist-deep water to try and get to him before he could reach the deep water.

I grabbed the big bass just in time. Pure luck. There is no way I could have landed this seven-pound bass on that rotten line. That evening at camp, I replaced the rotten line on my reel while the camp ranger and I had baked bass for dinner.

THEY'RE MISSING

A few weeks after my bass-on-the-gravel-bar story, we had a Scouting activity we called The Exploring Weekend. About 120 young men and women between the ages of 14 and 17 and their adult advisors were camping at Hohn Scout Reservation.

Our activity leader was a local conservation officer, and each Explorer Post brought special food items for the feast and was responsible for one of the activities. The activities included over a dozen events, like wilderness camping, outdoor cooking, archery, fishing, trapshooting, and target practice with .22 rifles.

The program Saturday evening included a huge outdoor wild-game feast and a dance at the pavilion. For dinner, we had pheasant, venison, quail, wild hog, fish, and barbecued raccoon. Steamed corn on the cob, roasted potatoes, watercress salad, iced tea, and pop rounded out the menu. The dance started around nine that evening and ran until a little after midnight.

It was about 1 am when a concerned volunteer leader said four of his crew were missing. The two boys and two girls had left the dance around 11 pm and had not been seen since. This can be a very scary situation.

Shortly after we started to search for them, we heard voices down by the lake and saw flashlights coming up the hill. The hunt was over and all were safe and accounted for. They had gone night fishing. It was a struggle to get their quarry up that long hill. They had tied into a 40-pound paddlefish/spoonbill. Our conservation agent showed them how to clean the critter and we ate it for lunch the next day. It was a great way to end the week.

TROUT FISHING AT BENNETT SPRINGS

About a week after our Exploring Weekend, I took a day off to go check out Bennett Springs, one of Missouri's four trout parks. You needed a trout tag that cost about a dollar a day back then.

The gentleman at the counter said that I might want to reconsider fishing due to the flood. It seemed they had a huge downpour, and the spring and the Niangua River were out of their banks.

I walked back to my car in the upper parking lot. The water was clear, but he was right; it was too fast and too deep to wade, and even the lower parking lot was under water.

All of a sudden, the light came on as I saw swirls on the surface of the flooded lot. Hatchery fish that had swum out of their ponds were feeding on some bugs in the lower parking lot. Yay!

I went back to the lodge, bought a trout tag, and—using a small mosquito pattern—had my limit of 12- to 14-inch rainbows in less than an hour. This seems a little silly now; but, back in the 70s, it was fun.

FARIBAULT, MINNESOTA

While living in Faribault, Minnesota, I found some super spots where no one else seemed to be fishing. It was 20 below zero one February morning when I hit a special spot where the Cannon and Straight rivers merge just below the Faribault Woolen Mills. There was about a foot of ice covering the Straight River.

The water from the Cannon River goes through the woolen mill to cool its equipment and exits at about 70 degrees. The big, deep pool where the rivers came together was full of fish just waiting for me to show up.

In two hours, I caught about 25 fish. I was using gigs, moving them up and down. I could see the walleye and sauger following my gig. They tended to hit it on the way up. I took home three 20-inch walleye and one big northern pike.

Another hot spot turned out to be a little spring creek that flowed into the Cannon River near Northfield, Minnesota. It took me two years to find this little gem.

It was only fishable for about two months of the year. By the time June would come around, the stream would be totally covered with thick duckweed. What made this place so cool was its population of BIG brook trout.

A conservation officer said the creek had the highest growth rate of any trout stream in the state. Try to imagine a spring-fed stream you could jump across populated with 12- to 14-inch brook trout. This was a special little place.

The White River in Southeast Minnesota and its tributary, Beaver Creek, also left me with some fond memories. The White yielded some small rainbows and a few large browns. One brown measured 21 inches.

I also did a little ruffed grouse hunting there. It took me a whole box of shells to get my first two grouse. They jumped up, flew low through the trees, and gave me one of my most memorable challenges.

Beaver Creek also tried to do me in. It was opening day, 15 degrees, with two feet of snow on the ground when I started fishing. My equipment froze and it was miserably cold as I trudged upstream into a winter wilderness. It was tough fishing. I caught one small brown trout and two small brookies in a small spring branch about a mile from my car.

The temp rose to about 25 degrees by two in the afternoon. I stood there looking at my little creek that was now a small river due to quick snowmelt. I had to cross it to get back to my car. A fifteen-foot-wide body of water turned into thirty feet, and the depth of the stream went from two to three feet to as much as four or five feet.

I needed one good yard to make it across the frigid water when the gravel washed out from under my feet. I threw my pole up the bank and jumped. Needless to say, it was a very wet and cold hike back to the car after emptying the water from my waders.

There are a number of other Minnesota rivers that left stories to be told. The Manitou runs into Lake Superior just north of Duluth. Take an old dirt road for several miles into the back country until it stops at an old railroad trestle, park the car, and hike down the tracks for about 45 minutes to an old iron bridge.

About two hundred yards above the bridge, there is a series of three waterfalls. I sat on a boulder at the base of the lower falls one September and caught 51 brook trout out of that one hole. Most of them were 4 to 8 inches. I had about five fish in that 10- to 11-inch range.

THE BEAR

The Nemadji River hits Superior just south of Duluth. I was told that steelhead ran up the river to the mouth of the Black Hoof River. The Black Hoof was supposed to be a good steelhead spawning ground.

I parked my car by the bridge, put on my waders, and hiked upstream to the Black Hoof. After several hours of fishing, all I caught was five little rainbow/steelhead. Because the stream seemed to take a big curl back to the south, I decided if I went over that ridge I could save a bunch of time getting back to the car. It worked.

As I reached the confluence of the two streams, I was handed a minor shock. There they were. Large BEAR tracks heading upstream right on top of my boot prints.

The muddy water was still oozing up from the bear's tracks. I carefully waded across the main river and hiked back to the car, looking over my shoulder just in case it was following me. I got to the car, took off the waders, grabbed a Dr. Pepper and walked over to the bridge. I leaned on the bridge railing and popped open my can of pop.

There he was. I was about fifty yards from the car and the bear was about fifty yards from the bridge. He grunted and started to run. I dropped the can of pop and ran like hell.

I had left the passenger front door of the car open. The cooler was on the floor there. I leaped into the car knees-first and caught the door with my hand.

Bang! Bang!

The first sound was the door shutting. The second sound was the bear denting the door. He proceeded to rip off the mirror and windshield wiper. When he stood up bashing the car, I could not see his head. He was huge.

I crawled over to the driver's seat, started the car, and took off. As I shot down the highway, I could see the bear in pursuit for a short time. I was lucky.

The next day I had to explain to my boss what I did to the Boy Scout council leased car. I don't know if he was angry when I explained what happened, or if he was secretly laughing inside. I might mention we were allowed to use our leased car for personal miles, but we had to reimburse the council so much per mile.

SANIBEL ISLAND

S anibel is an island near Fort Myers, Florida. Back in the 1980s, we had the opportunity to spend a week on this island. The food was great, the Gulf water was warm, and I had one unique fishing experience.

I started with a freshwater rod and reel with eight-pound test line. I waded out into the Gulf to the third sandbar and started casting a white, silver-bladed, quarter-ounce rooster tail spinner.

After only a few minutes of casting, I hooked into a fish that ran nonstop for 100 yards, ripping off my line as I ran down the sandbar trying not to lose the thing. I got lucky.

Fifteen minutes later, I beached a 26-inch snook. After releasing my prize fish, I proceeded to get my line cut three times. The snook's gills were shredding my eight-pound test line. I made an effort to fix things.

I put a three-foot section of thirty-pound leader on the end of my light line. Late that afternoon, I fished where Sanibel and Captiva Islands are connected by a bridge. There was a large boom in the water where some dredging had taken place.

The snook had millions of large minnows or small shad cornered, and it was a madhouse for about an hour or so. A large number of snook would rush into the minnows, sending thousands leaping in all directions. My spinners had a field day.

Twenty-two snook between 14 and 24 inches were caught and released. I had to snip off part of my leader every few fish caught, due to their gills cutting into the thirty-pound leader.

Advice: Don't use light freshwater tackle in the Gulf. You need to be better prepared. Early one morning, I tried one more time to hit the sandbar area. I saw a school of three sharks swimming between the second and third sandbars. That was enough to get me to put the pole away.

BEN AND JENNY

When we were living in Faribault, Minnesota, I decided to teach my son Ben how to fish. I took him and a couple of friends to a small creek just outside of town.

It was full of creek chub minnows, some in that 8- to 10-inch range. I figured we could use worms and each kid would have a blast. I was wrong. They started piling up rocks, built a small dam, and proceeded to wade and play in their new little pond. I was the only one who fished.

A couple of years later, I took him to a beautiful little spring creek full of brown and brook trout. I wanted him to succeed, so I used live minnows. He missed a fish on the first cast. On the second cast, he caught a 10-inch brown. By the time it took to put another minnow on his hook, he was gone. He was in the car. I asked him what was he doing? He said, "I caught my fish and I'm ready to go home."

It turns out that Ben's not a fisherman. He loved dinosaurs and Dungeons & Dragons. I might also mention that we used to box with each other. He wore the gloves and I used pillows. It didn't hurt, but he caught me off guard and knocked me on my butt. Ben did take after me in one way:

he hit his sister in the head with a rock—though accidentally. My Eagle Scout son still plays games, is an artist, and is good with computers.

Jenny, on the other hand, had her own way of making life interesting.

Our family was having a picnic at a park near Faribault. She was only four or five at the time and wore a little red jacket. It was a nice place. Lots of trees, a big field, and plenty of wildlife. Jenny was playing in the field about fifty feet from our picnic table when someone yelled. A little four-point buck didn't like the red coat.

Jenny fit snugly on the deer's head between its antlers. It hoisted her off the ground twice before a young man grabbed the deer by the antlers and Jenny dropped to the ground. Everyone was OK, but it was a scary situation. It turns out the deer had been raised by the park ranger and was not afraid of people.

A few years later, I needed to put a new roof on our old house in St Paul. I was three stories up and tied to the chimney for safety, when I heard a voice say, "Hi, Daddy!" My eight-year-old daughter was high up in the top of a tree, swaying back and forth on a skinny branch. She was level with me. I slipped and was saved by my rope. She laughed. I yelled for her to get down out of that tree. She just had no fear of high places.

When Jenny was in high school, we lived in Fargo, North Dakota. She went winter camping with her Explorer Post. It was cold, with about two feet of snow on the ground. They tent-camped, cooked dinner, and started on a late-night cross-country ski trip.

The joke is, we all went. But while they had skis, I was at the end of the line, walking in their ski-run tracks.

Under a full moon, we saw owls and coyotes and just had a great time. I need to also mention that Jenny melted the bottom of her boots by trying to warm her feet at the campfire.

Later that summer, her Explorer Post floated the Crow Wing River. This outdoors-enjoying environmental unit surveyed the river, logging things living in and around the water. That was one of the only times my second wife Janice went tent-camping. We were part of the adult leadership of this group. Janice likes to fish, but thinks you need to sleep in a bed, not a tent.

A FEW THINGS NOT SO FUNNY

I recall four times in my life when my children scared me.

The first occurred while living in family housing at Southern Illinois University. It was my turn to get up in the middle of the night and feed Ben. I guess he was about six months old at the time.

I got up from the kitchen table, put the bottle down, and started toward his crib when my foot caught a chair. I fell forward. Poor Ben went flying down the hallway and slid into the wall. He screamed, I cried, and my wife Mary, the ROCK, comforted both of us. We survived.

The second incident was when Ben started to walk and pulled a freshly-poured cup of hot tea off the table onto his chest. This brought on a quick trip to the ER. Again, we survived.

Jenny's problem when she was little was that she never walked, she *ran* from one spot to the next. We were on a day hike on a high bluff overlooking the Mississippi River between St. Paul and Minneapolis. I told her to stay away from the edge of the cliff and to stop running. Five minutes later, she ran by me. I yelled "Stop!" and she slid right up to the edge.

She did the same basic move in the Black Hills of South Dakota. We were climbing the steps of a huge fire tower so we could see the buffalo grazing on the prairie below.

The sign said *Walk, don't run. Climb at your own risk.*

I need to mention that I am afraid of high places and would normally not do this.

Jenny walked up the first third of the tower before starting to run. Again, I yelled, "Stop!" as she ran by me. She fell, slid on the wood floor right up to the chicken wire fence. Her face, hands, and legs went through the fence. Her butt stayed on the tower floor. Once again we survived, but not by much.

THE BLACK HILLS

There is a lot of history to take in and many beautiful, interesting places to see in the Black Hills of South Dakota.

We left Fargo, North Dakota, early in the morning and made it to the Bad Lands in South Dakota just before dark. We tent-camped there for two nights. We went hunting for dinosaur bones and found some.

On the third day, we moved to a campground deep into the Black Hills, near a manmade lake. I caught a few brown trout that morning below the dam, but it was late that afternoon when the real fishing started.

We stopped the car just outside the town of Custer, at a bridge that crossed a creek you could hop over and that ran through a meadow. There was a trout swimming in the little current under the bridge.

There was a bait shop just fifty yards from the bridge. I went in to buy some crawlers and asked the owner who owned the field by the bridge. He said he owned about seventy-five yards of stream just below the bridge.

He gave me permission to fish, but doubted there was anything in that ditch worth catching. We were looking for dinner and found it. In less than a hour, I had my limit of fish on a stringer and returned the unused worms to the store owner. He was amazed. He grabbed a pole, took our worms, and was fishing off the bridge by the time we started back to camp.

It pays to check out the smallest bodies of water. You never know what lies beneath the water's surface or what lurks within an undercut bank. Small places can yield big rewards.

MINNESOTA AND WISCONSIN

Camp Wilderness is the long-term summer camp for the Northern Lights BSA Council headquartered in Fargo, North Dakota. It consists of several thousand acres in Minnesota surrounding a large lake.

I showed up the week after camp closed and decided to do some fishing. I had light trout gear and three rooster tail spinners. Needless to say, my four-pound test line was in trouble. I will keep this short.

I hooked into a bunch of northern pike off of one point between the main lake and a much smaller one. I landed three of them before their friends sheared off my roosters. They weren't monsters, but plenty big enough to do my line in.

The three pike I landed were 30, 32, and 34 inches in length. I almost had a fourth one, but he leaped high and away from me at close range and snapped my line, stealing my last rooster. It was exciting and a bit of a physical and mental drain at the same time.

During this same time frame, I trout fished in a few streams in Wisconsin. The Kinnickinnic near River Falls had a good wild brown trout population in its lower reaches, with wild brook trout in its headwaters.

Browns in that 12- to 16-inch range were quite common. The White River in the Chequamegon National Forest also had a good brown and brook trout population. I would suggest not going fishing there during the late-fall bear season. Bears, bow hunters, alcohol, tent-camping, and fishing in the wilderness by yourself can be a problem.

A SECOND SECRET PLACE

In 1984, I was fortunate to get the Scout Executive job in Joplin, Missouri. This was a real special time in my life for a number of reasons. It took me a year or so to find what would be another secret place.

There were two spring creeks, one a tributary to the larger stream. A total of twelve miles of A+, wild, un-stocked rainbow trout water made this a special place. I built a relationship with local farmers that gave me the opportunity to fish this very special body of water. Each fall, I pass out Boy Scout popcorn to each landowner as a thank you.

I caught and released 103 rainbows on this creek one October in 1985. In 2019, I broke that old record with a 131 rainbows. Rainbows from 3 inches to 24 inches and everything in between made a normal day's fishing. A 26-incher was the largest trout I have caught and released on this creek.

Try to imagine your 3-weight fly rod bent over with a 20-plus-inch wild rainbow leaping four feet through the morning fog—that's what happens in this special place.

DAWN'S FISH

There was, and still is, a trout pond below a spring at Childress Scout Reservation near Joplin. I took my mom and sister Dawn there back in the mid-1980s, with the idea that anyone could catch a fish there.

My assumption was correct, but it came with an odd and special memory. Each person caught a fish, but it was Dawn's second trout that caused a ruckus.

Mom was sitting on the old picnic table and Dawn was fighting her 15-inch rainbow. I netted the fish, took the fly out of its mouth, and told her to hold it gently over the net lying in the pond for a picture.

She made a good attempt, but when the fish flipped, she lost her balance and did a head-first dive with her fish into the pond. Mom laughed so hard she cried and wet her paints.

JENNY'S DAY OFF

Here comes another short fish story. When Jenny was in junior high, she complained that she never got out of school like lots of other kids. Their parents took them out for special things, like weddings or short trips.

The next week, I gave Jenny an envelope to give to her teacher. The teacher read the note and asked Jenny if she knew what the note was about. She said she didn't.

Her teacher laughed and said, "You won't be in school tomorrow. Your dad is going to take you fishing."

We got up the next morning and were on a trout stream by 8 am. She caught three trout and I caught five fishing behind her. It was the third fish that made her and my day.

Jenny was standing in the middle of the outlet to a nice little pool when she hooked an 18-inch wild rainbow.

The line zipped off the drag. I told her to keep a tight line in case it jumped.

It jumped.

This spotted marvel leaped high into the air. The trout came down with a huge splash and ran right between Jenny's legs. The pole followed suit. Jenny was bending over double when I picked her up and turned her around. A few moments later we took a quick picture and released her fish.

It was a great day off.

PRAYER

D o you believe in prayer? My wife Mary came down with breast cancer at age 29. The doctor told me after the mastectomy that the cancer had spread to her lymph nodes, and with luck she had perhaps a year.

Ben and Jenny were both very young at that time and had no idea of what was going on. I prayed every night for another day with my soulmate.

At the end of year one, there was no cancer showing up. Eight years after surgery, she was still cancer-free. A few months later, this dreaded thing showed up again, and I lost her two years later.

I was hurt and angry with God for some time. Why did he have to take her from us? Then it dawned on me. The prognosis was for one year. God gave us ten.

A SECOND CHANCE

As these stories float along like life, things change. Time passes.

My son Ben was in the Army and my daughter Jenny was in high school. I was a single dad and working my butt off trying to bring our Scouting program to over 4,000 kids in our little eight-county Mo-Kan Area Boy Scout Council.

From September to late November, I made Scouting talks to first through fifth grades in about a dozen schools. You pass out flyers announcing a sign-up night, and do your best to get boys excited.

It was the week before Christmas when I received a strange Christmas cardfrom a second-grade teacher in a class where I'd made a presentation.

The school secretary had told the teacher I was single. Her card said if I ever wanted to catch a movie or dinner, to give her a call.

Jenny rolled her eyes and I pitched the card into the trash can.

A week after Christmas, I went to empty the trash can and found the card on the floor. Was it fate? I missed the can. I decided to send a note back, saying if she wanted to get together to give me a call. Forty-eight hours later, I got a note that said I was the one that needed to call.

Jenny was really doing the eye-rolling when I called the mystery lady and set up a date for the upcoming Friday night. Thursday night, I got a call from her saying she had to cancel our get-together. Her babysitter was sick.

She has a kid? I asked how old her child was. She said he was ten. I said that I had a fourteen-year old daughter who could do the sitting. She said Okay.

As I waited for the doorbell to ring, I told Jenny that this was probably a 300-pounder that could not find a date any other way. That was mean of me to say that. The doorbell rang. I opened the door and, behold, a five-foot-six, 118-pounder with reddish brown hair stood there with her son, Nathan. Janice was gorgeous.

We dated for several months. I even talked her into getting up at 3 am and took her trout fishing on the North Fork River. She caught some nice ones.

We were married 30 days before reporting to a new position in Fargo, North Dakota. Life has a way of giving us lots of options. We have been together for the last thirty years. Thirty good years.

THE FIRST 90 DAYS

Thirty days after our wedding, Janice, Jenny, Nathan, and I moved to Fargo, North Dakota. My new position as the Scout Executive of the Northern Lights Council was a huge responsibility and very scary. I had a new wife and two children living in a motel for months while I was trying to get a grip on a council that was in physical, emotional, and financial trouble.

The Northern Lights was a geographical monster. On top of my new job, I had to deal with a family situation that was a leftover from the previous five years.

There was a multi-year membership program through the North Central Region BSA. Scout Executives who earned the recognition received a week-long trip to Europe along with their spouses. My spouse had passed away and my daughter Jenny was given permission to take her mom's place. This was all set up six months before Janice and I got married.

The actual trip took place shortly after we moved to Fargo. To run off to Europe with your daughter while leaving your new wife in a motel with her son just doesn't sound or look good. But, somehow, it all worked out. The trip went fine.

We saw the Matterhorn, Lake Lucerne, and ate food we couldn't identify at a banquet. While traveling by bus, I saw people trout fishing with long bamboo poles. They used a fly and a cork. I saw one 15-inch rainbow caught this way. It didn't look very exciting.

On the home front, Janice and Nathan survived and so did the Boy Scout Council.

Back home, we left the motel and rented a duplex for a while. We eventually bought a house on the south side of Fargo. It sat on two acres. We had critters running through the yard and good neighbors. It was a great place.

MONTANA HIGHLIGHTS

My first of many trips to Montana started with Nathan's Boy Scout troop in Fargo, North Dakota. There were three patrols of Scouts in the troop and each patrol got to plan their own high adventure trip.

Nate's patrol chose to go where one of the older Scouts' patrols had gone the year before. They chose to take a week-long backpacking trip to the Absaroka-Beartooth Wilderness in Southeast Montana and Northeast Wyoming.

There were seven Scouts and two adults traveling in two vehicles. Going up and over Red Lodge Pass was a little scary. It had sharp curves and it was a long way down. I think I had a little altitude sickness for a short time.

I tried to explain to two fifteen-year-olds and five thirteen-year-olds that they couldn't hike eight plus miles each day. It was their plan and they said it was doable.

It was around 10 am when we hit the trail at about 9,000 feet. By nightfall, we were miles short of their goal. They were sore, tired, and making noises like they wanted to go home. We pitched camp, built a fire, and proceeded to freeze our tails off.

The next morning found frost, a frozen plastic cup of water, and a nice warm fire as everyone slowly got themselves up. I hinted that if they wanted to quit and go home that was their right, but how will they explain giving up on day one to the rest of the troop back home?

We looked at our map.

I told them, "You are only a mile from Granite Lake. What if we went there, made camp, and sat there for a couple of days? We could hike, fish, and get our heavy packs off our backs." They reluctantly chose to give it a try.

It was a great trip. Brook and rainbow trout were caught in Granite Lake and Lake Creek. After two days' rest, we hiked a half-day to a high mountain lake full of cutthroat trout. While there, they climbed 11,399-foot Lonesome Mountain, the highest peak in the Beartooths.

Two days later, we made it back to the parked vehicles. Our Scouts had conquered the wilderness. We made it through freezing nights, hot days, and one super nasty thunder, lightning, and hail storm. Our Scouts learned how to freeze-dry food, build a good menu, cook over the open fire, and catch their first fish.

One item of little interest, but that reflects what kids do sometimes, occurred on the long drive home. A van full of girls passed us several times. They waved and made faces at each other. Our van was passing them when one boy in the back of our van mooned the girls. I don't recommend this, but it happened.

Nathan and I made the trip into the Beartooths several more times. We went with friends, old Scouts, uncles, and Nate's future wife, CJ. He was in his twenties the most recent time.

One day on Lake Creek, just above Granite Lake, we caught 51 trout between us. We were using a mosquito dry fly pattern. I would go back again, but at 74, it might be more than I can handle.

ZERO HERO AWARDS

U p north, they treat the cold a little differently than those of us now living in Springfield, Missouri. It was a freezing 20-below-zero one February evening when we arrived at Anderson Scout Reservation near the St. Croix river.

There were about 25 Scouts and leaders in our group. We had rented a cabin and were well-prepared for winter camping. Several of the older Scouts informed our Scoutmaster that they were going to earn another Zero Hero award.

This means you have to camp out in a tent or snow shelter, etc. for 24 hours and prepare two meals during this time frame. It was about 1 am when Mr. Waugh, our Scoutmaster, came to me and asked if I thought we should pull in the older Scouts.

It was 20 below out and the wind chill made it more like 30 below. As we made our way to the door of the cabin, in came the older Scouts. The senior patrol leader said, "We ain't stupid. It's getting nasty out there." By breakfast time, the wind calmed down, but we were still sitting at 15 to 20 below.

This is when my 11-year-old son Ben came to Mr. Waugh and said he and two other 11-year-olds were going to earn their first Zero Hero award.

Mr. Waugh said, "Don't you think you guys are a little young for this first attempt?"

Ben said, "Don't worry, my dad will go with us."

I was screwed. Here's how it went down. Two feet of snow covered the ground when the four of us went out. We dug to the frozen ground under the snow.

Two old tents were placed in the hole flat to the ground. We placed our sleeping bags on the tents and then covered the bags up with two more heavy tents. A hot fire was started and we crawled in for the night. A plastic sled filled with small chunks of cedar wood was set close so I could pull the string and pull it up to me so I could throw wood on the fire without getting out of my sleeping bag. It worked like a charm. We survived the night.

Lunch and breakfast were another story. Our hot dogs were frozen stiff. One Scout tapped a dog on the side of a fence and it shattered like glass. We survived on mushy hot dogs and soup. When our 24 hours were up, we went into the cabin and ate hot food. We were whooped.

A number of years later, it was Nathan's turn to earn the award. It was only 3 below and there was no wind. For some reason, it seemed much colder than my earlier 20-

below experience. We built a snow shelter and dug in for the night. I had a hard time sleeping while Nate slept like a log.

About two in the morning, I had to pee. I got up and went out to water a tree. When I came back, Nathan was still sleeping like a baby. Enough! I woke him up and said, "How come you get to sleep and I'm freezing?"

He laughed, reached down into his sleeping bag, and pulled out one of those large hand-warmer things. He said, "Here, Dad, this will help you sleep."

He was right. Sometimes our children are smarter than us.

SIBLINGS

M om and Dad, for some reason, liked the letter D. If this was not the case, why did they name us kids Dean, Dawn, Donald, and Deanna? I mention us siblings in the order we were born, even if Dawn and Donald are twins. She came first. Deanna showed up some 13 years or so after the twins.

It was obvious, if you had chores to do, that you needed to be smart. The twins fought all the time. So, when it came to doing dishes, I washed. Two hours later, they were still snapping each other with the drying-towels.

When it comes to fishing, Donald knows where the secret place is in New Jersey. He also caught a big brown trout in a small tributary of the Musconetcong River one year. I think his best fishing was on my other secret wild trout stream in Missouri. He caught around thirty rainbows that day, with the largest measuring 21 inches.

Dawn's early fishing experience highlight started at the old tunnel where a small creek ran into the old Raritan canal. I told her she was too close when I tried to cast. She didn't listen and got hooked in the back of her head. I think we had to make a trip to see old Doc Hiner to have the hook removed.

I don't remember ever fishing with Deanna, but she did help me catch night crawlers one time. You could water the lawn and just pick them up off the ground. The hard way took a little longer. Some water with hot mustard mixed in it was poured down the worm holes. Worms don't like it at all. It only takes a minute or two to get them up and out of their holes. You need to rinse them off before putting them in your worm box if you want them to survive.

One final thought. Deanna makes great pizza and other Italian stuff. She can also give you a haircut or a perm.

FISHING IN COLORADO

The Flat Top Wilderness and the Conejos River in the San Juan Mountains are two of my favorite western fishing places. It has been many years since I visited the Flat Tops.

I know we hiked about 10 miles from the end of a dirt road to the back side of the mountains. We hiked along a small creek that was full of fish. Halfway in, I fished while my brothers-in-law, nephew, and his wife-to-be hiked off for a half-day hike. It was spectacular.

My three-weight fly rod and a prince nymph had a field day. The first pool yielded three cutthroat and two brook trout. I watched the end of my fly line jerk forward across the water's surface on my first cast into the second pool. Wham, a 15-inch cut came flying out of the water. It went on this way for about two hours. Thirty-five fish was my total catch of the day.

Two days later, while most of the crew tried to cross the Devil's Backbone, I fished one of the small high country lakes near our camp site. I caught one nice cutthroat. For some reason, I didn't have the right bug.

My nephew's girlfriend took a spinning rod and pitched a rooster tail into the lake and caught the biggest fish of the trip, an 18-inch cut. Yes, I was out-fished by a girl, but it was fun anyway. We had fish for supper that night.

The Conejos River in the San Juan mountains near Platoro has lots of different fun challenges for those of us who love to fish. The river has browns and rainbows, some in that 20- to 21-inch range. They have to be over 15 inches to keep one.

The tributaries are full of brook and cutthroat trout. My brothers-in-law, Ed, Mike, and Mark, and their friend John were hikers. They hiked the mountains while I fished the creeks and beaver ponds. I have visited this area three times in the last 10 years.

I convinced my youngest, Nathan, to take some vacation a few years ago. It was just the two of us. We rented a cabin in Platoro, Colorado, and fished our guts out. We also ate steak and potatoes and lots of other good stuff. Nate is a good cook.

It was on this trip that we spent a day some fifteen miles from our cabin, fishing a wild cutthroat trout stream. I think we caught about forty cuts in that 8- to 13-inch range.

Some years before this trip, I had a scary encounter on a section of this same stream. I had heard stories about mountain lions. I was the only human for miles. I had moved up a small canyon-like area with rock walls about 20 to 30 feet tall.

It started to rain, then sleet. I was releasing a gorgeous 14-inch cut when the water started to turn cloudy and was gushing over the little waterfalls in front of me. I had to get out.

Have you ever tried climbing up a stone wall with chest waders on while carrying your fly rod? Not much fun.

I made it up the hill and snuggled up against a large pine tree, trying to avoid the sleet. I was wet and cold. Suddenly something moved in the thick brush. It very slowly moved ever closer. It was quiet for a few moments. Then it moved a little closer.

If you are alone in the wilderness, wet, cold, and facing a mountain lion, and you don't have a gun, prayer might help. Then it happened. The little deer stepped out of the bushes, looked me over, and continued to finish its lunch.

I got up and started the long walk back to the car, still looking over my shoulder just in case there was something there.

FARGO, NORTH DAKOTA,
FISHING AND HUNTING

F argo sits at the southern end of what was old Lake
Agassiz. This ancient body of water ran from the
Fargo area all the way up into Manitoba, Canada.

This huge, somewhat shallow body of water nowadays is
a long, flat farming area. They grow lots of beets there.
The Red River of the North drains this area for 500 miles
to Lake Winnipeg in southern Canada.

I didn't do a lot of fishing in and around Fargo. There was
a small lake south of town stocked with brown and
rainbow trout. The only other serious fishing occurred on

Lake Sakakawea in the western part of the state. Two 24-inch salmon were caught while trolling the lake one fall. Now that I think about it, I also caught a few walleye and smallmouth bass in the Missouri River within the city limits of Bismarck, the state capital.

The following spring, I was invited by a couple of fellow Rotarians to float the Little Bighorn in Montana. My flies only captured two 14-inch browns. I think I seriously irritated my host of pure fly-fishers when I pulled out a rooster tail spinner and had a field day. They never asked me to go with them again.

One memory that stands out in reference to North Dakota is pheasant, partridge, and goose hunting. None of it came without a price. It was cold, wet, snowing, and often gave me terrible leg cramps.

You see, if you're hunting when it is 15 degrees and there are two feet of snow on the ground, you wear your chest waders to keep you warm and dry. Moving through deep snow by yourself with no dog to help you find the birds is a real pain.

On one such expedition, I hunted for three hours and saw nothing. Tired and hungry, I drove 20 miles down a dirt road to a small town just north of Lake Sakakawea. This little community only had a hundred yards of paved road, a granary, gas station, post office, school, two houses, and a restaurant.

What a joke. There must have been a hundred pheasants running up and down the street around the granary. They were pheasants, not chickens. I grabbed some home cooking at the restaurant and asked the manager if there was any good place to hunt near town? She said to check with the mail carrier and that he would be in shortly for lunch. I did.

It turns out the mailman was the husband of the restaurant manager. He said there was a large number of pheasants along a hedge row about a mile south of town. I asked who to contact for permission. He said go ahead, it was his farm. Long and short, I had my limit of pheasants and two partridges in less than an hour.

I plucked and gutted my birds in the cold by my car, and placed them in a cooler. An hour or so later, I arrived at the hotel in Minot, North Dakota, where we were to have our monthly BSA board meeting.

Note: Don't finish cleaning your game birds in the tub of your hotel bathroom. It makes for one heck of a significant bloody mess.

To complete this little section on hunting in North Dakota, I have to cover one unbelievable goose hunt.

John was my Program Director in charge of our camping and outdoor programs. He grew up in North Dakota and told me stories of huge flocks of geese and great hunting.

We went to the Devil's Lake area and spent the day driving all over the place. There were no significant geese on the lake itself, so we just kept driving all the back roads, etc.

Late in the afternoon, we came upon a small back country lake that was completely covered with about 10,000 snow geese. We stopped and just sat there. I asked John why we were just sitting here.

He said, "You can't hunt after 1 pm. Just wait and watch."

One by one, family groups of geese took flight and headed south. John started the car and followed the flights as best he could. An hour or so later, and ten miles down a number of dirt roads, we came to a huge farm field that had recently been harvested. Thousands of geese were circling and landing in the field. It looked like a white tornado. It was dinner time.

We drove down the road another couple of miles and found a farmhouse and asked permission to hunt there the next morning. The farmer said no. Deer hunters put a hole in his house last year. John noticed the name on the mailbox. I don't remember the name, but when John asked about it, the farmer said, "Yes, that's my son." The conversation went on from there. It turned out his son was John's roommate in college. He laughed and said, "Go ahead. You can hunt."

We came back early the next morning, dug holes in the field, put out white and black plastic bags on sticks. We sat in the holes covered with straw and waited. John said that if they are not bothered, the geese will return to the exact spot where they ate the night before.

It was just getting light enough to see when we heard the honking in the distance. They were coming, thousands of them, circling and landing right on top of us. I think the limit was 15 birds. I had 11. I don't know how many John had before he ran out of shells. As we were cleaning up our hunting area in the field, the birds were still landing about a quarter of a mile from the spot where we were hunting. This was without a doubt the best one-day goose hunt I have ever experienced.

EXPLANATION OF THE HUNT

I carried my waders, fishing pole, and 12-gauge in the trunk of my car. This was due to me traveling hundreds of miles each week to cover our huge council service area.

If you are on the road for days and going two or three weeks without a day off, you use any spare time you can to relax. That means hunting or fishing if and when you can.

We rotated these board meetings between Fargo, Bismarck, Grand Forks, and Minot. Geographically, the Northern Lights BSA council covered the state of North Dakota, two counties in Montana, and South Dakota, plus 18 counties in western Minnesota.

My position as Scout Executive made me responsible for a professional and clerical staff of about 20 people. We served 4,000 volunteers, and around 12,000 youth and their families. The hardest part of the job was to raise over a million dollars from scratch each year to keep the program going.

SPRINGFIELD, OUR FINAL DESTINATION

In 1994, I accepted the Scout Executive position in the Ozark Trails Council headquartered in Springfield, Missouri. Ozark Trails came about due to a merger between the Mo-Kan Council in Joplin and the Ozark Council in Springfield.

This new 31-county service area had about the same population as the Northern Lights Council in Fargo, North Dakota. My wife said she was tired of 30 below zero, three feet of snow, and mosquitoes the size of small birds. It was time to move south.

I held this position until retirement in 2012, thus ending a 40-year career with the Boy Scouts. When you like your job, it doesn't seem like work. It becomes a mission and gives you a chance to make a positive difference in the lives of thousands of kids and their families.

I might also mention that the BSA also serves girls. The Venturing and Exploring programs have been around since the 1970s and nowadays girls can be Cub Scouts and Scouts. 2020 will see the first young ladies earn the rank of Eagle Scout. We have come a long way since 1910.

BACK TO FISHING – 2

I believe those of us living in the Springfield, Missouri, area have some of the best fishing in the country. The Elk River, Big Sugar, James River, Big and Little Piney, Meramec, Jacks Fork, Gasconade, and Niangua are just a handful of the great smallmouth bass streams in the state.

The Lake of the Ozarks and Table Rock Lake have super crappie, smallmouth, and largemouth bass populations. Walleye are also in these bodies of water. Fellows Lake, just north of town, has all of the previously mentioned fish plus a significant population of muskies over 40 inches in length. All of our major rivers and lakes also have blue and channel catfish, bluegill, and goggle eye.

The North Fork of the White River and the Eleven Point are unique bodies of water. They are great to float, swim, and seriously fish. The North Fork of the White has wild rainbow trout, stocked browns below its large springs, and smallmouth bass throughout its entire length. I own twenty acres on the river. My catch-and-release fishing includes a 22-inch rainbow, a 25-inch brown, and a 20-inch smallmouth. There is also a significant walleye and striped bass population that comes up out of the North Fork Lake in the spring.

The following memory is in reference to the previously mentioned 25-inch brown on the North Fork.

It was early spring and the river was about four feet higher than normal but still clear.

My eight-ounce rooster tail stayed on the surface in the high fast water, so I went to a quarter-ounce rooster to try and get down deeper. There was some moss flowing in the swollen river. It had a tendency to get caught on my line, making a fish seem bigger than normal. I had a couple of 14-inch rainbows that felt like 20 inches.

I tossed the big rooster across the river into an eddy and let it drop to the bottom. I think he hit my spinner before it reached the bottom. He was slow and heavy as he moved downstream. I figured I had lots of moss on my line and on the fish. I slowly worked this dude upstream, being careful not to overdo my four-pound test line. The fish was still deep and only about twenty feet away from me, when it flew to the surface.

This big brown came about three feet straight up over my head, flipped wildly, and hit the water like a ton of bricks. He ran again. I couldn't follow him due to high water. I had also forgotten to bring my landing net. I was in trouble. I was also very lucky. After about ten minutes, we were both tired. I gently trapped him between me and the bank, measured him, and carefully released him into the swollen river.

The Eleven Point is a spectacular smallmouth stream. There are wild rainbow trout in its headwaters, plus the state stocks rainbows for several miles below the larger springs.

Try this for a half-day of fishing. On a chilly January morning last year, I found myself with waders on and standing in two feet of clear water below one of the larger springs.

The temp got up to 45 degrees by 10:00. The early morning mist glowed with the first rays of sun as a mink scooted through the root wads on the far bank. A bald eagle gave me a good looking-over and an old turkey gobbled away deep in the woods.

I was using my favorite lure, a 1/8 ounce dark brown rooster tail spinner. On my first cast, the rooster was whacked by an 18-inch smallmouth. He leaped out of the water and dove deep. It was a good battle.

My rooster nailed seven smallmouth in my first seven casts. It took about fifteen minutes before I caught and released my first rainbow, a chunky 15-incher. I fished for four and a half hours that frosty morning. My catch totaled 84 smallmouth, 31 rainbow trout, and 2 chain pickerel, for a total of 117 fish caught and released in four hours of fantastic fishing.

I need to explain how this works. In the winter, when the Eleven Point starts to freeze on its edges, gobs of minnows and crayfish congregate in the big pools below the largest springs. One of these springs dumps an average of 222 million gallons of 58-degree water per day into the main river. This one spring makes up 60% of the river volume in the winter months.

The trout and smallmouth congregate in significant numbers following this intense concentration of minnows and crayfish. You can be bringing in a nice smallmouth and watch 3 or 4 other bass trying to take the spinner out of its mouth. It really helps if you know the stream.

You need to know when and where to go. In reference to chain pickerel, I can only say they are somewhat rare, but it's interesting to catch one now and then. The two I caught were 12 and 19 inches.

PS: Update. I just came back from the Eleven Point 11/10/2020. I caught 116 fish today: 10 rainbows and 106 smallmouth. My two largest fish were both 20 inches, one rainbow and one smallmouth.

There is one more super type of fishing here in Missouri not yet mentioned: farm ponds. I still have the key, given to me in 1984 by a volunteer Scout leader, to the front gate of his eight thousand acre farm.

In order to irrigate his fields, he has two large farm ponds about a mile apart. The old pond is about 20 acres. The newer of the two is about 30 acres. It was on these two ponds that I set my so-far all-time total daily fish catch record. One spring in 2015, I started at daybreak and fished until 4:30 in the afternoon. I caught a total of 216 fish.

I use a fish counter I call my clicker to keep track of things. The breakdown went this way: 112 largemouth bass, 96 crappie, and 8 sunfish. Boy Scout's Honor!

The largest crappie was 14 inches. The largest bass was 25 inches. I caught 12 bass in the 20- to 25-inch range. I would guess the largest bass weight was in that 8- to 10-pound range. I kept some crappie but released all the bass. I bet there are bass tournament fishermen that don't have that kind of luck. It was a great day on the ponds.

Another short pond story took place on a 17-acre pond called Cowan Lake. We held a Key 4 meeting at our council commissioner's farm. The four of us fished in the morning and held our Boy Scout council planning meeting that afternoon.

Our president and I fished together in an old row boat. He had little or no experience fishing, so I was in teaching mode. With some guidance, John caught 47 bass, crappie, and sunfish on a rooster tail in about three hours. We had a fun time.

John went home and told his wife he had caught more fish in one morning, with the help of the Fish Whisperer, than he had caught in the whole rest of his life added together. His wife replied, "Oh, you caught two!"

THE COWS

T he cows also messed with me. I had permission to fish a small wild trout stream not far from home. The farmer said to drive through the gate and that I could park by the creek. This saved me a good deal of extra walking.

It was a good morning. My three-weight fly rod and a copper john fly caught about a dozen wild rainbows. One was a super-pumped-up 22-incher that jumped at least three times before entering my net. After a couple of good hours of fishing, I headed back to the car.

I reached the field by the creek and my car was gone. There was nothing but about 40 dairy cows bunched up in the middle of the field. Then I saw a glimmer of some bright red. The cows had my car surrounded. They were licking the crap out of it with their big, long, sticky tongues and making swirls all over it with their heads. They had small horns. Yes, my car had been severely SLIMED.

This story ends with me trying to explain the damage on my red Windstar to my wife and the insurance company

Note: Don't park red vehicles next to cows.

MY #1 COLLEGE FOOTBALL GAME

There are some events that are just cemented into our memory. I have always had a tendency to root for the underdogs.

On January 1st, 2007, my wife and I sat down to watch the Fiesta Bowl. Janice grew up in Oklahoma and was a hardcore Oklahoma Sooners fan. I didn't say much at the time, but I was hoping that undefeated Boise State would somehow let the world know that even the little schools should have a shot at a National Title.

It was kinda like the college system wanted to prove they were right by not letting Boise play for the National title. They would have nationally ranked Oklahoma crush them on national TV. I am not sure I remember this correctly, but it was a thriller going back and forth and didn't end until the fifth overtime. Boise won 43 to 42.

I yelped and clapped my hands and my wife gave me the evil eye and left the room. It was and still is my favorite college football thriller.

ALASKA

I have been to Alaska twice: once on a cruise, and once a land expedition. The cruise was nice but could not compare to the eleven days Janice and I spent wandering from one place to the next.

We ate great food, pulled the pump handle off the pump at a gas station when I forgot to pull it out of my car, and caught a bunch of fish. We rented a car, spent two nights free at a Boy Scout camp, did the all-day Denali bus tour, saw bears, wolves, moose, foxes, and some eagles.

We took a boat tour to see glaciers. This was also an all-day deal. Whales, seals, and thousands of different kinds of birds were flying among the cliffs and glaciers. Some of the glaciers were so blue and clear. It was like looking at colored glass.

Our favorite town was Talkeetna. We ate reindeer sausage and blueberry pancakes that were 16 inches across. Yum.

The fishing was also super. For $50, I had a fella take me up the Susitna River from Talkeetna to a clear stream that entered the main river on our left. I stood in one spot for over three hours and caught 34 salmon on a white rooster tail spinner. There were thousands of fish there, stacked up like cord wood.

I brought the lure in fast and on the surface so I would not snag them. It worked like a charm. I was told they sometimes ate pieces of white dead salmon meat floating in the river. These fish ran in that four- to six-pound range.

The following day, Janice and I used a guide and his boat to catch silver salmon. This was a food trip. You could keep three fish per person. There were four others on this guided fishing trip. One by one, they caught fish.

We were using a green and white stringy-type wooly fly. Everyone had their limit except me. I had only caught two 10-inch arctic char that I released. I was afraid I was about to be out-fished by my wife, another lady, and her three kids, when my luck turned. My three silvers were about 25 inches and perhaps as much a six or so pounds. The guide service processed our fish and sent them back to our home in Springfield, Missouri.

Perhaps my most remembered fishing hour came on a creek called Honolulu Creek near Talkeetna. Janice and I stopped by the highway bridge. No one was there, but you could see a few huge king salmon below the bridge. They were swimming but looked like they were on their last legs.

My wife agreed to wait in the car while I just wanted to take a few casts. You know how that works. There is no such thing as just a few casts. In the first few minutes, I hooked and released two 18-inch rainbow trout. A few hundred yards upriver, I ran into another big surprise: arctic graylings. Six of these beauties in the 14- to 16-inch range hit my rooster tail and were released.

It was at this point, when I had been out about forty minutes, that I noticed two things. I could not see the road or the car, and there were gobs of bear poop and huge bear tracks everywhere. This was probably the first and only time I ever showed up early to my car.

PETS

O ur pets are warm, loving creatures. They are our friends. They keep us company and give us the tender loving care we all need, especially when we are alone or experiencing problems. The following covers some of my pets and their stories.

Jingles was half-collie and half-German Shepherd. Dad brought him home in a shoe box. He looked like a big ball of fur with two little eyes, pointy ears, and a wagging tail. Dad saved him. The lady who owned him raised show dogs and she considered Jingles to be an accident. We named him after Jingles P. Jones, a character on a TV western in the early 50s played by Andy Divine.

Jingles had a rough life. He looked like a lion. He had a collie mane and the short-haired body of a shepherd. He was huge, strong, and always in trouble.

He ran into things in the house, breaking enough stuff that Mom had Dad turned him into an outside dog. He broke the rope that was attached to the tree. The rope was replaced with a heavy chain.

Jingles hated trains. It only took him about a week to break the chain. He leaped over the backyard fence.

Dragging eight feet of heavy link chain, he ran down the tracks toward Trenton, chasing a freight train.

A neighbor called the next day and said she saw a dog that looked like Jingles walking on the tracks near the Trenton train station, nine miles from our house. A call early the next morning from another neighbor said there was a dog that looked like Jingles crawling on the rail road tracks. He was coming home.

I know mom was a little afraid of Jingles, but she went after him by herself. She picked him up and carried him home. Mom took him into the kitchen, removed the chain, washed off the soot, and put medication on his sore legs and feet.

It was decided we had to do a better job of taking care of Jingles. My Dad and Uncle Gobe built him a big, safe, and comfortable house in the back yard. No more ropes or chains. His house was big enough for me to crawl in with him. The pen was huge, with a wire roof, sides, and floor covered with a foot of dirt.

I will end this story with the following info: Jingles and I spent time running and playing in the woods. We knew the train schedule and made sure he was in his pen when trains came by. He was the first to greet me when I came home on leave from the Air Force or college break. Jingles was my friend. He lived to be 21 years old.

Another set of pets that did not have the best ending were Molly and the Goldfish Triplets.

Molly was a calico cat that was rescued by me and a friend just before a kitten-drowning party in the river. (That was how my friend's dad got rid of unwanted kittens.) I hid her in my bedroom until Mom found her. Mom was a sucker for a good story and let me keep her. She slept in my bed every night. She was lots of fun.

The goldfish were on sale a few months later and we bought three of them. They lived in a fishbowl on top of our old radio. The radio was about three feet tall. We listened to the "Lone Ranger" and "The Shadow Knows" long before we had a TV.

One morning, one of the triplets was missing. Molly was on top of the radio staring at the two remaining fish. Two days later, number two was gone. Molly had her paw in the bowl messing with number three.

We kept Molly in my bedroom to protect the fish, but number three also disappeared. A few days after the departing of the last goldfish, the old standing radio went on the blink. Dad opened it up to replace a blown radio tube and found three cooked goldfish.

The theory is that the vibration of the radio caused the fish to jump out of the fish bowl. They fell down inside the radio, and got fried on the hot radio tubes. Molly was an innocent bystander.

Henry Ert was named after my Dad. I don't know whose pet he was. This bright yellow, blue, and green parakeet just hopped around his cage, sang a little, and ate lots of seeds. Dad and Mom left the door open sometimes so Henry Ert could fly around a little. He even enjoyed riding on an old model train in the basement. It was good exercise.

For some reason he didn't eat for a couple of days. He just stood on his little perch or swing and watched us. It turns out he had croaked. He died standing upright on his swing. That was the end of bird pets.

Seaweed the cat liked to fetch the little round rings that came off of the milk jugs. This cat would play this game all day if you let her. She would even bring them to me and toss them into the filled bathtub in an effort to get me to play.

This same fun-loving cat tried to eat my daughter. Jenny, being little, didn't yet know how to handle a cat gently. One night we heard a moaning sound coming from Jenny's bedroom. I went in and found the cat getting revenge. Seaweed was on top of Jenny, biting her on the face. I fixed the door so the cat couldn't get in her bedroom and taught Jenny how to hold the kitty nicely.

After Seaweed, came cats C-2, Fizz Gig, and New Cat.

I might take a moment to mention Pip the pheasant eater. This was a two-year-old English setter that was given to me by some neighbors who were moving out of state.

She found the pheasants ok, but grabbed the birds I shot and ran away with them. She would have them half-eaten by the time I could catch up with her. I eventually gave her to a kid that lived on a farm and wanted a dog. He was sure he could train her to do the right thing. A few weeks later I found out she ate his dad's white chickens, a whole bunch of them. I am not sure about the fate of Pip. ?????

When Janice and I got married in 1990, she had Macho. He was a big, white Shih Tzu. He was terrified of thunderstorms. We came home one evening after a movie to find dog poop all over the floor and stairs. We tried to keep him in the bathroom when we went out, but he chewed a hole in the bathroom door, trying to escape from the thunder.

Snuggles followed Macho, who was in turn followed by Pebbles.

Pebbles was one great puppy. This little Shih Tzu was perhaps the most loving, gentle critter we ever had. She sat in my chair with me each night and watched TV. She loved to play and was a big part of our family. It was like having another kid in the house. She cornered a skunk in the back yard once. We were lucky. Everyone made it out alive. Pebbles lived with us for about 12 years before passing.

I end my pet stories with Miss Kitty. She showed up at our house and was scared of everything. Someone dumped her outside when she was only a little black ball of fur. She hid under our flowers until we captured her and had her fixed and vaccinated.

Janice said we were not going to have an inside pet until she got another dog, so Miss Kitty was an outside cat until the snow came. Now she has a house on the front porch, one in the garage, and, in bad weather, one in the hallway. She is my kitty. She loves me and Janice. She helps me work in the garden, water flowers, and clean the pool.

She does have one very bad habit. My wife feeds the birds. Miss Kitty caught one of Janice's hummingbirds and brought it to the front door as a present. That did not go over well.

One night last fall, Miss Kitty grabbed an opossum by the tail while it was eating her dinner. The opossum won the tug-of-war by totally ignoring the cat. I captured the not-

so-smart-opossum and released it 10 miles down the road
so it could bother someone else. Miss Kitty is now three
years old and doing fine, as long as she leaves the birds
alone.

A QUICK UPDATE ON THE KIDS

Ben now works for the postal service, Jenny works for the local public library system, and Nathan is a Baptist minister in Texas. Both Ben and Nate are Eagle Scouts. Jenny spent several years in the Exploring program. Scouting made a positive difference in all of our lives.

GRANDCHILDREN

J anice and I have four grandkids. It's too bad they all live in Texas. It's an eight-hour drive one way.

The oldest is about to go to college. She is a super swimmer and might get a free ride some place. She will also be a great cook and desserts will be her specialty.

Our oldest grandson excels in water polo and plays a tuba in his school marching band.

Our youngest grandson plays football and is also a great swimmer.

Our youngest granddaughter is also a swimmer. She likes to draw. I think she will become a great artist someday.

Like most kids, they squabble and get under each other's skin. I used to gently hold onto them when they were going too far and pretend I was asleep. I called this Pop Pop Prison. I hope those points of friction go away as they get older.

They all like games and certain TV shows and movies. We taught them how to play cards. They are getting better at playing pinochle and hearts. I also don't want to arm wrestle my oldest granddaughter. Swimming has made her one super-strong young lady. I think she might beat me.

JOEY AND ONE LAST FISH STORY

My nephew Joey is a super-nice guy. He and his wife work hard to support their family, including an army of kids and dogs. He needed a break.

He flew to Springfield from Philadelphia and we spent several days fishing and eating yummy stuff. We hit the Eleven Point, The North Fork, and my two favorite bass and crappie ponds. I asked him how many fish he thought he would catch. He said he hoped he wouldn't get skunked. The Eleven Point gave him five rainbows and four smallmouth on our first morning.

That afternoon, the North Fork added another six rainbow and a brown trout. His biggest trout was about 16 inches range. Before we hit the ponds, I talked him into setting another one-day goal. He started with ten. I said, "Too low." He then said twenty. I told him 40 would be a low number.

Once again, using our rooster tails, we hit the ponds at daybreak. His first cast brought in a 14-inch bass. By 10:00, he passed his goal of 40. Joey ended up with 67 bass and crappie. A five-pounder topped things off just before lunch.

We quit fishing a little after noon and drove into a small town to Cookie's Cafe. They make everything from scratch, including 26 different kinds of pie.

It was a great day.

PRESENT DAY ACTIVITIES

It is October 2020 at the time I'm writing this, and we are all dealing with the upcoming presidential election and this cruddy COVID-19 pandemic. We are wearing masks, using the pickup service at the grocery store, going through the drive-up window at Hardy's and McDonald's, and fishing at least once a week.

I can hit any number of good streams, rivers, lakes, or farm ponds. It's nice, because I'm usually the only one there.

My fridge is full of crappie, channel catfish, and walleye. I'm still letting all the bass and trout go free. Catch-and-release is the only way you can keep our WILD TROUT streams alive and healthy.

FISHING TIPS

I think I will throw in a fishing tip or two just for fun. I tend to most always fish moving upstream. If the trout are facing into the current, they are less likely to get spooked. I use this point of attack with both flies and spinners.

I can get down deep where the big guys are. I have watched big rainbows look my offering over but not hit it. If I let the rooster or fly hit the bottom and jerk it up and down, they often will hit it. I think they see it as a crayfish or big stone fly. It works.

If you don't get hits moving up, drop a shot down or across the stream and move it real slow. I pick up stragglers that way. All of my spinning reels have a 6-to-1 gear ratio. This keeps me from getting hung up on the bottom in shallow, fast water. I have saved a number of spinners with this tactic.

Last but not least, have you ever tried fishing for big largemouth bass and crappie with a fly rod? Inch-and-a-half green and white streamers or small jigs work well in big farm ponds. Stone flies draw in the smallmouth on the big rivers.

WHAT IS A FISH WHISPERER?

When kids or non-fisher people ask me what a Fish Whisperer is, this is what I tell them.

A Fish Whisperer walks up to a pond, stream, or lake, places their pointer finger in the water, and twirls it in a fast circle, making lots of ripples. All the fish in the area can feel this movement through their lateral line that senses vibration. They know what it means: "OH CRAP. The Fish Whisperer is here." And they know they only have two choices:

#1, Everyone pick a number and line up and bite. If they do, I catch lots of fish and I let them all go.

#2, Give me a hard time. If they do, I fish harder and still catch some of them. And I will take some of those fish home and eat them.

The truth is, if you know how to read a body of water and have the right fly or lure, you can have a great day.

CATCH AND RELEASE

I was recently asked by a friend if I really talk to my fish. The answer is "Sorta." I know I have looked at good-looking water and said to myself, "I know you're there." I have spotted fish and dropped that perfect fly and said, "Take it, take it." There are those fish, like some big rainbows, browns, cutthroats, and a 10-inch brookie, that have been told they were great fighters, or just how beautiful they were, as I released them back into the stream.

One fish holds a special place in my memory.

While fishing my secret place here in Missouri for wild rainbows, I caught a beautiful 18-inch rainbow. She was gorgeous. While she lay in my net recuperating, I clipped a small "V" in her dorsal fin and then released her. About a year later, in about that same area, I caught a 21-inch rainbow with a "V" in her dorsal fin. I made another small "V" and released her. The following spring, I was fishing some three holes upstream from the area where I had caught my two-time rainbow. A huge rainbow shot out from the undercut bank, whacked my stone fly, and came leaping out of the water three times before entering my net. She was a huge 24-incher. It was her. I placed my third "V" on her dorsal fin and released her for the last time.

Catch and release is extremely important, especially when it comes to WILD fish. I have been told that if a big female rainbow lays 10,000 eggs, only two of those fertilized eggs will ever get to be her size under normal conditions. Let her go. Enjoy what she brings to you and others in the future.

FINAL THOUGHTS

The following is a dream I had when I was 38 years old. We lived in St. Paul, Minnesota, at the time. I was working hard and getting in a little fishing when I could.

This is a recurring dream that popped up about six or seven times over a couple of weeks. Being now a 75-year-old Fish Whisperer, I think this story is worth telling.

It was one of those bright sunny mornings in the fall. The leaves were falling and I felt that urge that says, "Let's go fishing."

I arrived at the Kinni (Kinnickinnic) in Wisconsin at about 10 am. I pulled my waders up, grabbed my fly rod and WALKER, and headed for the creek.

It took a while to navigate that 20 feet between my car and my favorite pool. My walker and I stopped in about 12 inches of water and dug in for that first cast. I flipped the fly under the bridge, at least I think it was my fly.

The strike came quickly. The monster rainbow sucked in the fly, came flying out of the water, dove deep, and dashed downstream. It was at this point in my dream that I think I had an out-of-body experience.

There I was, lying face-down in the river, still holding onto the fly rod.

A young man and his girlfriend appeared out of nowhere and said, "Look, this old geezer had a heart attack."

The boy picked up my fly rod because he could tell there was a fish at the other end. It was a real let-down when I watched him take a six-inch SUNFISH off my line and release it.

That was all I could take. I woke up, rolled over, and hoped that this would not be how this Fish Whisperer's story would end.

Thank You.

THE END

ABOUT THE AUTHOR

I grew up on the banks of the Delaware river in New Jersey. Fishing and hunting were the things that I enjoyed as a young man. Life's experience in school, the USAF, college, and 40 years working for the Boy Scouts of America have all helped to create the man I have become. I hope my book and the many landscape and seascape paintings I have produced will bring joy to others and inspire others to follow their dreams.

www.ingramcontent.com/pod-product-compliance
Lightning Source LLC
Chambersburg PA
CBHW061211170626
46809CB00003B/1316